AF608190

THE CATHOLIC UNIVERSITY OF AMERICA
CANON LAW STUDIES
No. 191

MARRIAGES OF CONSCIENCE

AN HISTORICAL SYNOPSIS AND COMMENTARY

by

VINCENT PAUL COBURN, A.B., J.C.L.
Priest of the Archdiocese of Newark

A DISSERTATION

Submitted to the Faculty of the School of Canon Law of the Catholic University of America in Partial Fulfillment of the Requirements for the Degree of Doctor of Canon Law

THE CATHOLIC UNIVERSITY OF AMERICA PRESS
WASHINGTON, D. C.
1944

Nihil Obstat:

Ludovicus Motry, S.T.D., J.C.D.,
Censor Deputatus.

Washingtonii, D. C., die 26, *aprilis,* 1944.

Imprimatur:

✠ Thomas Josephus Walsh, S.T.D., J.C.D.,
Archiepiscopus Novarcensis.

Novarci, die 26, *aprilis,* 1944.

The Catholic Protectory Press

ARLINGTON, NEW JERSEY

DEDICATED TO

MARY

THE MOTHER OF GOD

TABLE OF CONTENTS

CHAPTER VII

CHAPTER VIII

CHAPTER IX

CHAPTER X

FOREWORD

The Supreme Sacrifice of the Son of God on the Cross opened to all mankind the sacramental channels of Divine Grace which Christ had instituted during His earthly life for the future sanctification of all men. From the beginning of the Christian era the reception of the Sacraments has been the most perfect manner in which man could effectively progress in his path back to God. Being God, Christ did not leave the care and administration of the Sacraments to chance, but He placed the sacred trust of bringing these instruments of grace to men in the hands of the Church He had founded. Through all the centuries of her remarkable history the Church has displayed the greatest solicitude in protecting the dignity and sanctity of the Sacraments, but, obedient to the will of her Founder, she has made every effort to make the reception of the Sacraments always possible to worthy persons. The ecclesiastical legislation now in force regarding Marriages of Conscience is an excellent example of the Church's safeguarding her sacred trust, but, at the same time, employing every device to make one of the Sacraments readily available to persons who would experience serious difficulty in attempting to receive this Sacrament of matrimony in the ordinary manner. Permission to enter a Marriage of Conscience may only be granted in extraordinary cases, and the exceptional regulations supplied in the law for such marriages must be strictly observed in each instance. The purpose of this work is to trace the history of the Marriage of Conscience, and to elaborate, in some detail, on its meaning in the present law.

It is impossible to arrive at a full, correct understanding or evaluation of the law now regulating Marriages of Conscience without some knowledge, at least summary, of the gradual development of this institute through the centuries. This is true, because the present legislation finds its sources in former enactments, and represents a successful attempt to fuse the important points of previous legislation with the more specific provisions and additions of modern legislators. However, the history of this institute herein presented is not calculated to be exhaustive or detailed, for the reason that history is neither exclusively nor primarily the concern of this work. The method adopted is to present, for the most part, the principal regulations developed over the years as they appeared in the documents of the most outstanding authorities who have interested themselves in exposing the thought and legislation of their times in reference to strictly secret marriages. These persons were Gratian, Gregory IX, and Benedict XIV. Each gathered the worthwhile existing enactments of their times and attempted to incorporate their findings into specific pronouncements. They did this with increasing success.

The Marriage of Conscience did not officially appear in the external forum till the middle of the eighteenth century, but it had its origin and reason for existence in the clandestine marriage, which was a valid form of marriage till the time of the Council of Trent. Initial concern, therefore, will be given to a consideration of the history of the clandestine marriage until it became outlawed, then the internal forum substitute for strictly secret valid marriage will be treated, and, finally, the establishment of the Marriage of Conscience in the external forum will be recounted with its attendant legislation which remained in force till the promulgation of the Code of Canon Law.

The canonical commentary, which is essentially the more important part of this work, is a detailed interpretation and application of the presently binding legislation regarding Marriages of Conscience. No attempt has been made to present the general marriage legislation of the Church, which must form the background for a correct understanding of the regulations herein delineated, since to include it, even in brief form, would make the work unnecessarily cumbersome, and would serve no real purpose. Knowledge of general marriage laws is easily obtainable from reading the pertinent law itself, and from perusal of one or more of the several excellent commentaries. The first chapter of the canonical commentary is devoted to clarifying the concept and meaning of the Marriage of Conscience in the present law, and defining its scope. The succeeding chapters expose and explain the law itself on this subject. Final consideration is given to related questions and practical difficulties which may arise in actual cases when use of the Marriage of Conscience is justified.

The writer wishes to take this occasion to express his sentiments of profound gratitude to the Most Reverend Thomas Joseph Walsh, D.D., J.C.D., Archbishop of Newark, for the opportunity afforded him for graduate study and to the Most Reverend Thomas Aloysius Boland, D.D., Auxiliary Bishop of Newark, for his kindness and constant encouragement. The writer wishes also to acknowledge his deepest appreciation for the kind consideration, and invaluable assistance extended to him by the members of the Faculty of the School of Canon Law.

PART ONE

HISTORICAL SYNOPSIS

CHAPTER I

HISTORY OF THE CLANDESTINE MARRIAGE BEFORE GREGORY IX

ARTICLE I. THE MARRIAGE OF CONSCIENCE DIFFERS FROM THE CLANDESTINE MARRIAGE

THE Marriage of Conscience as it exists in the present Code of Canon Law has a relatively short history, having been established only two hundred years ago by Pope Benedict XIV (1740-1758).[1] However, it had its counterpart in the clandestine marriage which is of ancient origin. In fact, the encyclical of Benedict XIV was aimed directly at eliminating the abuses of the clandestine marriage by proposing a thoroughly adequate and legal substitute.

Marriages of Conscience are those which are celebrated in the form prescribed by law, but in such a manner that they remain secret. The banns are not published,[2] and the priest assisting and the witnesses are bound to secrecy[3] as long as the parties desire it and place no act liberating the local Ordinary from his promise of secrecy.[4] Clandestine marriages in the present legislation are those which are invalid because of lack of form.[5] Previously to the Council of Trent,

1 Ep. encycl. *Satis Vobis*, 17 nov. 1741 — *Codicis Iuris Canonici Fontes cura Emi Petri Card. Gasparri editi* (9 vols. Romae [later Civitate Vaticana]: Typis Polyglottis Vaticanis, 1923-1939 [Vols. VII-IX *ed. cura et studio Emi Iustiniani Card. Serèdi*], n. 319. (Hereafter this work is cited as *Fontes.*)

2 Canon 1104.

3 Canons 1105; 1107.

4 Canon 1106.

5 Ayrinhac-Lydon, *Marriage Legislation in the New Code of Canon Law* (rev. ed., New York: Benziger Bros., 1940), p. 236; Vermeersch, *Theologiae Moralis, Principia—Responsa-Consilia* (3 ed., 4 vols., Romae:

however, in the times of Gratian and of the Decretalists two types of secret marriage were regarded as valid. In the first group were included those unions which were contracted with some of the circumstances public, for example, the *sponsalia de futuro,* but not completely perfected in the manner desired by the Church authorities. These were presumed marriages and valid if the consent was true.[6] In the second class were placed clandestine marriages in the strict sense, or those which were perfected without any knowledge or approbation of ecclesiastical authorities, but which were likewise valid marriages.[7] The reason for this essential change over the centuries, in the substantial character of clandestine marriages was that the form now required for marriage was not then required.[8] In fact, before the Council of Trent no specific form was required as a condition for the validity of the marriage.

Università Gregoriana, 1933-1937), III, n. 739; Vermeersch-Creusen, *Epitome Iuris Canonici* (5 ed., 3 vols., Mechcliniae: H. Dessain, 1933-1936, II, n. 383.

[6] C. 30, 31, X, *de sponsalibus et matrimoniis,* IV, 1; Potthast, *Regesta Pontificum Romanorum, inde ab A. post Christum natum MCXCVIII ad A. MCCCIV* (2 vols., Berolini, 1874-1875), n. 9661, 9662. (Hereafter this work will be cited as Potthast.

[7] C. 1, 8, 9, C. XXX, q. 5; c. 1, X, *de clandestina desponsatione,* IV, 3; c. 2, X, *de clan. desp.,* IV, 3; Friedberg, *Quinque Compilationes Antiquae* (Lipsiae, 1882), *Comp. I,* lib. IV, tit. 3, c. 2; *Comp. IV,* IV, 3, 3, (This will be the manner hereafter of citing passages from the *Quinque Compilationes Antiquae* pointed to in this work. All citations have been taken from the Friedberg edition.); Jaffé, *Regesta Pontificum Romanorum* (ed. 2, correctam et auctam auspiciis Gulielmi Wattenbach curaverunt F. Kaltenbrunner [ad annum 590], P. Ewald [anno 590-882], S. Löwenfeld [anno 882-1198], Lipsiae, 1885-1888), JL, n. 13774. (Hereafter in this work, documents written before the year 590 and included in Jaffé will be cited as JK, if written between 590 and 882 as JE, and if written between 882 and 1198 as JL, each document with its number as given in the *Regesta.*)

[8] Carberry, *The Juridical Form of Marriage,* The Catholic University of America Canon Law Studies, n. 84, (Washington, D. C.: The Catholic University of America, 1934), p. 4, 6.

Article II. Early Prohibitions Against Secret Marriages

Every law has a history of its own from the fact of its existence and from its purpose, which is usually to direct action that abuses might be done away with. The history of the circumstances which gave rise to a particular regulation affords a very helpful background for the correct understanding of the law in question. From the beginning of Church history the joining of the members of the Christian Society in marriage has always been looked upon as a public act.

St. Ignatius (✝ ca. 107) in the second century advises that all proposed marriages be made known to the Bishop. "It is becoming that marriage be contracted with the advice of the Bishop, so that it may be according to God and not according to concupiscence."[9] Early ecclesiastical writers were most anxious that Church members look upon marriage as a public act. However, it is important to note that they did not venture to condemn clandestine marriages as invalid, though this possibility was pointed out. The prohibition of Tertullian (160-223) is an early indication that such an attitude existed. "Among us secret marriages, that is, such as are not publicly professed before the Church, are in danger of being condemned as adultery and fornication."[10]

Precisely because of the dangers inherent in clandestine marriage, the Church took drastic steps to eliminate them in the Council of Trent by establishing a juridical form of marriage,[11] but it is remarkable enough that until that late date they were certainly recognized as valid marriages. St. Thomas insisted that the common opinion be admitted, which maintained that clandestine marriages were valid

[9] *Letter to Polycarp,* c. 5: "Decet vero ut sponsi et sponsae de sententia episcopi coniugium faciant, ut nuptiae secundum Deum sint, non secundum cupiditatem." — Migne, *Patrologiae Cursus Completus, Series Graeca* (161 vols., Parisiis, 1856-1866), V, 732. (Hereafter this work will be cited as Migne, PG.)

[10] *Liber de Pudicitia,* c. 4: "Ideo penes nos occultae quoque coniunctiones, id est, non prius apud ecclesiam professae, iuxta moechiam et fornicationem iudicare periclitantur." — *Corpus Scriptorum Ecclesiasticorum Latinorum,* (68 vols., Vindobonae, 1866-1936), XX, 225.

[11] Sessio XXIV, *de ref. matrim.,* c. 1.

according to the natural law, since consent, which had always been the required natural essential, was present.[12] A modern author, commenting on the attitude of pre-Gratian writers in the matter of clandestine marriage, asserts that, though these writers vainly attempted to establish the prohibition against clandestine marriages by alleging many canons of questionable authenticity, if they were not altogether false, they nevertheless set out in high relief the belief of their time regarding the validity of marriage celebrated without the priest.[13] The early Church, then, looked with displeasure on marriages entered into secretly, but refrained from condemning them as invalid. The development of this attitude and the legislation it provoked in the times of Gratian and the Decretalists will be discussed here.

It might be stated though, before any consideration be given to Gratian's treatment of the clandestine marriage, that the civil law of the early centuries reflected the attitude of the Church. In the Theodosian Code a special provision was inserted regarding prenuptial settlements which included a prohibition against secrecy, since it required marriage with the "knowledge of friends." [14] But, again, this does not argue for a strict condemnation of unions entered into without this circumstance. Further, "under Justinian (527-565), and for centuries earlier, any declaration of consent, in whatever form given, sufficed for legal marriage, *consensus facit nuptias.*" [15]

However, in the extensive christianisation of Europe, among the attempts of political leaders to eradicate abuses contrary to the social order, there was at least one explicit, thorough repudiation of marriages attempted without the prescribed form. Charles the Great, in the year 802, passed a law commanding that marriages be entered into with the priestly blessing, with sacerdotal prayers and oblations.

[12] In IV *Libros Sententiarum,* d. 28, q. 1, a. 3.

[13] Wernz-Vidal, *Ius Canonicum ad Codicis Norman Exactum* (7 vols. in 8, Romae: Universitas Gregoriana, 1923-1938, [Vol. V, *Ius Matrimoniale,* 2. ed., 1928]) V, n. 529.

[14] Krueger, *Codex Theodosianus* (Berolini: apud Weidmannos, 1923-1926), VII, 3.

[15] Leage, *Roman Private Law* (2. ed., London: Macmillan & Co., Ltd., 1930), p. 102.

Should this form not be followed the unions effected were not to be regarded as true marriages, but rather as adultery, concubinage or fornication.[16] Thus, in point of fact, civil legislation preceded ecclesiastical in outlawing clandestine marriages.

Article III. Regulations Found in Gratian

The Decree of Gratian (ca. 1140) was never approved by the Church as an authentic code of law.[17] Nevertheless it would certainly be a mistake to fail in placing the correct evaluation on this work, or to minimize its importance. Gratian is an excellent summary of ecclesiastical legal thought for the first eleven centuries, and the method employed in this decree introduced a new epoch in the science of Canon Law.[18]

The Fifth Question of the Thirtieth Cause of Gratian's work is devoted in great part to proposing norms and regulations to be used in dealing with clandestine marriages. Before all else, Gratian proposed a condemnation of secret marriages said to have originated with Pope Evaristus (112-121). There is no certain indication that Gratian considers this canon a declaration of the invalidity of clandestine marriages, but it seems that, unable to reach a definite conclusion on the force of this canon, he simply included it in his work, allowing readers and commentators to draw their own conclusions. But whatever may have been the view of Gratian on the Canon of Pope Evaristus, his general treatment of clandestine marriages seems to indicate belief in their essential validity, though he believed they should be avoided. This caution against secrecy, and the provision of ways of obviating the possibility of clandestinity in marriage, form the second norm placed by Gratian. The third point emphasized is the essential validity of clandestine marriages, based on the valid consent of both parties. Lastly Gratian elaborated the

[16] *Admonitio Generalis,* 23 martii 789, n. 68, repeated in *Capitularia Missorum item Specialia,* anno 802, n. 43—*Monumenta Germaniae Historica* (188 vols. incomplete, Hannoverae 1826—), Legum Sectio II, *Capitularia Regum Francorum,* tom. I, (ed. A. Boretius, 1883) pp. 58, 104.

[17] Van Hove, *Prolegomena ad Codicem Iuris Canonici,* (Mechliniae: H. Dessian, 1928), n. 191.

[18] Van Hove, *op. cit.,* n. 190.

manner in which valid consent in secret marriages could be proved by those on whom fell the duty of judging them. The discussion of these several recommendations of Gratian can more easily be continued under the four headings following, in the order outlined above.

A. The Canon of Pope Evaristus

As his first canon treating with clandestine unions Gratian proposed part of a letter said to have been sent to the Bishops of Africa by Pope Evaristus. This canon, as Gratian indicated in the summary preceding it, specifically forbade clandestine marriage. In an accompanying Gloss [19] his words are adequately explained to express prohibition. The reason was that marriages of this kind cannot be proved, and the Church does not render judgment regarding secret matters.

The author of the above mentioned Gloss stated that although "secret marriages should not be performed, nevertheless, if they are, they should be upheld." [20] He considered consent alone to constitute the substance of such marriages.[21] After defending the essential validity of secret marriages the Glossator proposed his own reasons for their prohibition. They may, in fact, be fornication, but under the species of marriage. Again, if following a marriage of this kind one of the parties changes his or her mind and a separation ensues, the remaining party would be left bereft of proof of the marriage. Here he again pronounced the reluctance of ecclesiastical authorities to render judgment in secret matters. A passage is cited in which married persons are excluded from sacred orders, but only when their marriage was known, not, therefore, if it was occult.[22] The judgment of these last was to be left to God, as it was in many other cases when proof could not be established.[23]

This canon of Pope Evaristus which declared clandestine mar-

[19] *Glossa Ordinaria,* pr. C. XXX, q. 5, s.v. *Quod autem.*

[20] "Utrum clandestina matrimonia debeant fieri; dicunt quidam quod non, si tamen fiant, tenent."—*Glossa Ordinaria, loc. cit.*

[21] "Cum huiusmodi solemnitates non sint de substantia matrimonii, sed sufficiat solus consensus."—*Glossa Ordinaria, loc. cit.*

[22] C. 2, D. XXXII.

[23] C. 20, C. II, q. 5; c. 7, C. VI, q. 1; c. 23, C. XXXII, q. 5.

riages adulterous, not true marriages, and alleged by Gratian, is a spurious one.[24] The original letter was a response directed to the Bishops of Africa, given on March twenty-fourth between the years ninety-seven and one hundred five. The text of the letter was distorted by the authors of the Pseudo-Isidorean Decretals to suit their own purposes,[25] and in this form it was incorporated by Gratian into his work. The corruption of the work indicated by Jaffé [26] is understandable in the light of the fact that the Pseudo-Isidorean Decretals were composed, in great part, with the intention of strengthening the hands of the Bishops against lay domination.[27] In the beginning of the canon in its altered form, the power of the Bishops, received from the Apostles, of demanding specific solemnities to be observed in the performing of marriage is asserted, thus emphasizing their supreme authority while sacrificing the authenticity of the letter itself.

The section of the disputed letter appearing in Gratian is as follows:

> "Aliter legitimum sicut a patribus accepimus, et a sanctis apostolis, eorumque successoribus traditum invenimus, non fit coniugium, nisi ab his, qui super ipsam feminam dominationem habere videntur, et a quibus custoditur uxor petatur, et a parentibus propinquioribus sponsetur, et legibus dotetur, et suo tempore sacerdotaliter, ut mos est, cum precibus et oblationibus a sacerdote benedicatur. . . . Ita peracta legitima scitote esse conubia; aliter vero praesumpta non coniugia, sed adulteria, vel contubernia, vel stupra, aut fornicationes potius, quam legitima coniugia esse non dubitate, nisi volunta propria suffragaverit, et vota succurrerint legitima." [28]

Gratian did not state his own opinion on the force of this canon. He seems rather to have withheld his own view as to whether these

[24] JK, n. 20 (spurious); Wernz-Vidal, *Ius Canonicum,* V, n. 626, footnote 5.

[25] Hinschius, *Decretales Pseudo-Isidorianae et Capitula Angelramni* (Lipsiae, 1863), p. 87.

[26] JK, n. 20 (spurious).

[27] Van Hove, *Prolegomena,* n. 163.

[28] C. 1, C. XXX, q. 5; JK, n. 20 (spurious).

statements, supposedly of Pope Evaristus, definitely declared secret marriages invalid. In the light, however, of the canons following this one, in Gratian's treatment of clandestine marriages, the conclusion must be that he believed they should be avoided, but that in point of fact they were valid once they were entered into with the proper will and consent.

B. Provisions Against Secrecy

Conceding the validity of clandestine marriages, but in express disapproval of them, Gratian quoted a ruling which he attributed to a sixth century Pontiff, to demonstrate that none of the faithful, whatever station in life they had occupied, could secretly enter into marriage. All were to be married publicly, and receive the blessing of the priest.[29] This canon has been adjudged a spurious one, however, it appears also, but in a more extensive form and under a different authorship in the Second of the *Quinque Compilationes Antiquae.*[30] In other canons the faithful were cautioned not to presume to marry without a dowry being properly arranged and without the marriage taking place in a public manner.[31]

The law of the Gospels was invoked in a canon which Gratian ascribed to Pope Leo in order to support the ecclesiastical disapproval of secrecy in arranging and performing marriages.[32] In each case formal *sponsalia* were to be contracted with the observance of all the solemnities required by the Church. In the event that these ceremonies were not observed the marriage was to be considered sin-

[29] "Nullus fidelis, cuiuscumque condicionis sit, occulte nuptias faciat, sed benedictione accepta a sacerdote publice nubat in Domino." — C. 2, C. XXX, q. 5; JK, n. 867 (spurious, but ascribed by some to Pope Hormisdas [514-523]).

[30] IV, 3, 2; *infra,* p. 13.

[31] C. 6, C. XXX, q. 5.

[32] C. 4, C. XXX, q. 5; Burchard, Ivo, and Anselm cited this canon as originating with Leo, but Saint Augustine was declared to be its author in the Council of Reims-Trosly-Breuil. Cf. *Corpus Iuris Canonici,* (ed. Lipsien. 2 post Aemilii Ludovici Richteri curas instruxit Aemilius Friedberg, 2 vols., Lipsiae: Ex Officina Bernhardi Tauchnitz, 1879-1881. Editio anastatice repetita, Lipsiae: Tauchnitz, 1922), pars prior, col. 1105, *Notationes Correctorum* to c. 4, C. XXX, q. 5.

ful. These regulations were contained in a letter to the Bulgarian Bishops composed by Nicholas I (858-867).[33] The prohibition under pain of sin was explained to affect only those who omitted all solemnities. This would no doubt have been the case in secret marriages. If one or the other of the ceremonies was not included because of some excusing circumstances then no sin was thought to have been committed.[34] Gratian, then, stating the attitude of the Church, urged that public ceremonies be used in contracting marriage, and accused those of sin who married in disregard of these prescriptions.

C. The Validity of Clandestine Marriage Was Based on Consent

In the Eastern Church, but not in the Western, there was a tendency to consider the nuptial blessing as something essential to valid marriage. Certain Greek priests had taught this doctrine to the Bulgarians, but Pope Nicholas I denied the truth of their teaching. In his reply to the Bulgarians he recalled the marriage ceremony as it existed at Rome. He did not admit that the religious ceremony with the blessing of the priest and the imposition of the veil was necessary for a valid marriage, but, on the contrary, insisted that consent of the contracting parties was, of itself, sufficient to constitute valid marriage.[35] Therefore marriage consisted principally in consent, which consent was not vitiated in any way by a physical separation of the parties. If then, after marriage, one would separate from the other, neither party could marry again.

For Gratian valid marriage, whether clandestine or public, was based on consent. In this he adhered to the opinion of the ecclesiastics of his day. He objected to a canon which explained the required formalities for marriage[36] on his own authority in these words, *"Multa sunt, quae prohibentur, quae si fiunt, ex post facto*

[33] C. 3, C. XXX, q. 5; JE, n. 2812.

[34] *Glossa Ordinaria,* c. 3, C. XXX, q. 5, s.v. *cuncta.*

[35] "Sufficiat secundum leges solus consensus eorum, de quorum coniunctionibus agitur. Qui consensus si in nuptiis solus forte defuerit; caetera omnia etiam cum ipso coitu celebrata frustrantur."—C. 2, C. XXVIII, q. 2.

[36] C. 8, C. XXX, q. 5.

convalescunt . . . Sic clandestina coniugia contra leges quidem fiunt, tamen contracta dissolvi non possunt; quia ex legitimo voto subsequente corroborantur." [37] The precise meaning of the words of Gratian in this place is obscure, since the subsequent promise did not seem logically to follow marriage already contracted. However, the insistence on the promise or consent as precluding any possibility of dissolution is unmistakable.

Roman Law, Gratian related, also affirms that marriages are valid if the formalities are omitted, as long as consent has been given. The passage cited is taken from the *Epitome of Julian.* There it is found that one becomes the legitimate husband of a woman by giving a promise while touching the Scriptures. But even though no book were used, and no dowry given, the woman would still be the legitimate wife in virtue of the promise. She would have a claim on the husband's property in the event of his death, and the children of this union would be legitimate.[38] It is clear, then, that for Gratian the validity of secret marriages depended, in the last analysis, principally on valid consent. Nevertheless, as is remarked in a Gloss accompanying Gratian's defense of the sufficiency of consent, the presence of true consent had to be proved.[39]

D. *Proof of Valid Consent*

One cannot deny, so Gratian explained, that clandestine marriages are valid, as long as the presence of true marital consent has been or can be proved. The reason for their prohibition lies in the difficulty encountered in establishing the fact of consent, especially if one or both of the parties should deny it. If both parties admitted that they gave true consent to one another there was little ground for doubt. In the event that it was uncertain whether consent was or was not given, no one could presume to give judgment.[40] Gratian left the decision in these uncertain cases to God alone; it was not

[37] *Pr.* C. 8, C. XXX, q. 5.

[38] Haenel, *Iuliani, Epitome Latina Novellarum Iustiniani,* (Lipsiae: prostat apud Hinrichsium, 1873), p. 92, n. 4.

[39] C. 8, C. XXX, q. 5, s.v. *Sed obiicitur.*

[40] "Quamvis vera sunt tamen credenda non sunt, nisi quae certis indiciis comprobantur."—1. *pr.* C. 9, C. XXX, q. 5.

the custom of the Church to decide in hidden matters, he declared.[41]

When the question of a secret marriage arose there was to be no immediate condemnation, but proof was to be sought.[42] The method to be adopted was to include the questioning of witnesses, a discussion of all the circumstances, and an evaluation of their influence on the disputed marriage. This was to be accomplished by asking questions and proposing objections so that both sides had an opportunity to shed light on the affair. Inquiry was also to be made as to whether anything had been passed over which should have been mentioned. These instructions were incorporated in a spurious letter ascribed to Pope Eleutherius, supposedly written between the years 174 and 189.[43] The *Glossa Ordinaria* contained a caution for the judge in cases of this kind to render his decision according to the facts brought forth in the case, not in accord with his own personal opinion in the matter.[44]

Upon presentation of one who was a witness to a secret marriage the judge could, if he liked, question the competence of the person to testify.[45] A witness could be rejected if his character did not merit that he be allowed to give testimony.[46] This was the case if the witness produced was himself a party to a clandestine marriage, since persons equally guilty could not testify for one another, as the canon just cited states. The interrogation was not to be a cursory one, but was to cover all circumstances and details of the disputed marriage.[47] One would hardly be able justly to determine the culpability in any matter, St. John Chrysostom said, by simply attending to the objective considerations the while one neglected to inspect the surrounding circumstances.[48] In fact, to insure the revelation of the whole truth in the matter it was recognized that there were

41 C. 2, D. XXXII; c. 20, C. II, q. 5; c. 7, C. VI, q. 1; c. 1, C. XXX, q. 5; c. 23, C. XXXII, q. 5.

42 C. 10, C. XXX, q. 5; JK, n. 21 (spurious).

43 C. 11, C. XXX, q. 5; JK, n. 68 (spurious).

44 C. 10, C. XXX, q. 5, s.v. *Ante*.

45 *Glossa Ordinaria*, c. 11, C. XXX, q. 5, s.v. *Cuncta*.

46 C. 18, C. II, q. 7; JK, n. 86 (spurious).

47 *Glossa Ordinaria*, c. 11, C. XXX, q. 5, s.v. *Et ordinem*.

48 C. 14, C. XXIII, q. 8.

cases when it was advisable to have the parties question one another. If this procedure was followed, then the persons involved had to take an oath that their questions would not give rise to calumny. This oath was not of course required if the judge himself proposed the questions.[49] Finally, when the testimonies were completed, the judge was to make himself certain that nothing had been omitted which should have been included in relating the facts of the case, inasmuch as his power of supplying for defects was quite limited.[50]

Gratian's expression of opinion regarding clandestine marriages and their treatment opened with their condemnation, based on a false source. Nevertheless he hardly believed in the canon of Pope Evaristus in its fullest sense himself, for while he advanced reasons for avoiding secret unions, yet he did not reiterate the declaration of their invalidity. Next he insisted that valid consent formed the foundation for marriage, public or occult. Lastly, the manner of testing and determining the validity of secret marriages after they had taken place was proposed. Before concluding Question Five of Cause Thirty, which was devoted in great part to supplying secret marriage regulations, Gratian in summary fashion offered his own opinion as to why they should be avoided.

> "Apparet clandestina coniugia ideo esse prohibita, quia, cum alter eorum coniugalem affectum se ad alteram habuisse negare voluerit, legitimis probationibus convinci non poterit; quibus deficientibus, iudicis sententia rite absolutus, reatum adulterii uterque incurrit, dum utroque eorum vivente aliis se copulaverint." [51]

Article IV. Developments from Gratian to Gregory IX

Most of the prescriptions regarding clandestine marriages appearing in the compilations between Gratian and Gregory IX were incorporated into Gregory's Decretals. However, there are two enactments of this era which cannot be found in the later Decretal

[49] *Glossa Ordinaria,* c. 11, C. XXX, q. 5, s.v. *Interrogandi.*
[50] *Glossa Ordinaria,* c. 11, C. XXX, q. 5, s.v. *Remaneat.*
[51] *Pr.* C. 11, C. XXX, q. 5.

legislation. The canon of Pope Hormisdas (514-523)[52] is repeated in the *Secunda Compilatio* of the *Quinque Compilationes Antiquae* under the name of Alexander III (1159-1181).[53] In its original form this canon forbade all, of whatever station in life, to marry secretly, but in the later edition a three year suspension was added for priests who were found to have blessed these secret marriages. This canon, with the addition, was simply attributed to Alexander III by the author of the *Secunda Compilatio,* no explanation or reason being given. The attribution has little historical probability; on the other hand it seems that Gratian repeated the canon as he found it in the works of his predecessors,[54] and with them ascribed it to Pope Hormisdas. However, since Jaffé quotes it among the letters of Pope Hormisdas, but as a spurious one,[55] the conclusion must be that the true source has as yet not been discovered.

Another canon of Alexander III, immediately preceding the one in the *Secunda Compilatio* discussed above, gave instructions on the manner of dealing with persons who went secretly to bishoprics other than their own to be married, in consequence of the prohibition of their own Bishop against the marriage. If such a union was invalid, the parties had to separate. If it was valid, the contracting parties were to be given a severe penance for their wrongdoing, but the marriage could never be dissolved.[56]

[52] *Supra,* p. 8.

[53] IV, 3, 2; JK, n. 867 (spurious).

[54] The form of this canon proposed by Gratian is identical with that found in the works of Burchard, Bishop of Worms (1002-1025), and Ivo, Bishop of Chartres (1090-1117).—Richter-Friedberg, *Corpus Iuris Canonici,* pars prior, col. 1105, *Notationes Correctorum* to c. 2, C. XXX, q. 5.

[55] JK, n. 867 (spurious).

[56] IV, 3, 1.

CHAPTER II

LEGISLATION IN THE DECRETALS OF GREGORY IX

Article I. Principles Governing Clandestine Marriages Found in the Decretals of Gregory IX

The first question considered by Gregory IX (1227-1241) with explicit reference to clandestine marriages was the necessity and manner of proving them. If after a secret marriage had taken place either party denied it, the burden of proving the fact of marriage remained with the man. *"Si quis clam desponsaverit aliquam, et mulier vel vir negat huiusmodi desponsationem; viro incumbit probatio."* [1] This enactment presupposed the validity of clandestine marriages. The claim to their validity had been previously demonstrated.[2] It also indicated in a more precise way how proof was to be established.

In a Gloss accompanying this law Bernard of Parma (✝ 1266) recalled the punishments incurred by blood relations who married secretly as had been previously detailed by Gratian.[3] These marriages were not to be regarded as legitimate. The contracting parties, witnesses, and all consenting to the union were *infames,* and as such none of these were to be permitted to give testimony in proof of the validity of any marriage, especially the marriage in question.

The burden of proof was placed on the man for several reasons. St. Augustine (356-430) was invoked as saying that man was the head of the woman, and that his responsibility was therefore superior to hers. Thus in committing adultery he sinned more gravely than the woman.[4] Moreover, if a woman claimed that she had never had carnal intercourse with a certain man, it was left to the man to

[1] C. 1, X, *de clandestina desponsatione,* IV, 3; *Comp. I,* IV, 3, 2.

[2] C. 8, 9, C. XXX, q. 5; *Comp. II,* IV, 3. 1.

[3] C. 4, C. III, q. 4.

[4] C. 5, C. XXXII, q. 6.

decide, since his authority was greater than the woman's.[5] In a more spiritual light man was the head of the woman, as Christ is the head of man. The crime of a woman who is not subject to a man was much the same as the crime of a man who was not subject to Christ.[6] This matter of leaving the proof of marriage to the man, without restriction, was not explained in the same manner by all, as is quite obvious, but the principle itself was never deserted.

An opinion appearing in a Gloss accompanying this canon of Gregory IX defined that, according to common understanding, the burden of proof was incumbent on the party by whom the marriage was alleged.[7] The accompanying *casus* is one wherein occult marriage had been entered. Later the man demanded that the woman act as his wife, but she denied the marriage. The man was then called on to prove the fact of the marriage. The same was true conversely; if the man denied the marriage, the woman had to prove it. If neither could or would prove the fact, then the marriage could be dissolved. A note was added to the effect that the solution offered in this case was an application of the belief of Bernard of Parma, though no explanation was given to explain why the principle applied for the solution of the case obviously contradicted the prescriptions of the canon itself.

A rather far fetched explanation of how the phrase *viro incumbit probatio* could be applied to both spouses was advanced by Hostiensis (✝ 1271).[8] In clandestine marriages, he said, if the man or woman denied the union, proof had to be supplied by the man, that is, by the one who alleged the marriage. If the man actually denied that the marriage was contracted, but the woman made it manifest that a contraction of marriage had taken place, then the woman assumed the mental stature of the man, and the man lapsed to the inferior state of the woman. Such a situation could intervene, he continued, inasmuch as women were sometimes called manly in view of their strength of soul and spirit, and, on the other hand, men were some-

[5] C. 3, C. XXXIII, q. 5.

[6] C. 15, C. XXXIII, q. 5.

[7] *Glossa Ordinaria,* c. 1, X, *de clan. desp.,* IV, 3, s.v. *Si quis.*

[8] *Summa Aurea* (Lugduni, 1580), lib. IV, tit. *de clan. desp.,* s.v. *Quare prohibeantur.*

times called womanish in view of their effeminate will and softness of heart. An exposition similar to this was given also by Gratian.[9] The explanation as proposed by Hostiensis appears somewhat bizarre, and perhaps he was not altogether convinced of its value himself, for he added at the end of his exposition that the suggested solution was a feasible one if witnesses could be produced, but that if witnesses were wanting the furnishing of proof was left to the man.

If there were no witnesses to testify to the fact of the marriage, so Hostiensis proposed,[10] but both spouses confessed that *sponsalia, either de futuro* or *de praesenti,* had been contracted, then as long as the man insisted that the espousals culminated in carnal intercourse he was to be believed, whether the woman admitted or denied it. His word likewise was to be accepted if he affirmed that he had not had carnal intercourse with the woman. Two exceptions were admitted against this rule. The first was that the word of the woman was to be taken if, after the avowal of the man that he had intercourse with her, she was nevertheless able to prove herself a virgin upon bodily inspection by medical men. The other case existed when someone sought to make a desired woman his wife, and to this end swore that he had contracted marriage with the woman in question by an espousal with words *de praesenti,* therefore inducing a valid marriage. Even if the man produced a witness in proof of such a marriage, if the woman denied the marriage, she was not held to it in view of the man's deficient proof.

The Decretals of Gregory IX obtained the force of universal law through their promulgation by means of the Bull *Rex Pacificus,* September 5, 1234.[11] Thenceforward, interpretations which extended the law beyond its substance could not be accepted. The conclusion to the first principle as proposed by Gregory IX regarding secret marriages had then to be that, if they were denied by either party, the obligation of supplying proof remained with the man.

The second point treated by Gregory IX dealt with the impossibility of granting a dispensation from secret marriages once they were entered, for either they could be proved externally to be valid,

[9] C. 6, C. XXXII, q. 6.

[10] *Loc, cit.*

[11] Van Hove, *Prolegomena,* n. 206.

or they remained secret and had to be regarded as unlawful unions. Toward the end of the reign of Alexander III (1159-1181), probably in the year 1181, the Bishop of Beauvais addressed an inquiry to him seeking powers to dispense from clandestine marriages. The Pope replied [12] that he was unable to determine what manner of dispensation could be used in that kind of case. If the marriage was so secretly entered that legitimate proof of it could not be established by witnesses, then the parties could not be compelled by the Church in any way. Of course, if the contracting parties wished to publish the fact, as long as no reasonable cause stood in the way, the marriage had to be accredited by the Church authorities, and it was to be approved as if it had been contracted in the eyes of the Church from the beginning.[13]

The reluctance of the Church to render judgment on things as hidden as clandestine marriages is cited by Panormitanus (1386-1453) as well as her ready approval of these unions when they became public.[14] In a case detailed in a Gloss accompanying this law of Gregory, the question was proposed as to what treatment should be given those who married secretly, precisely to avoid making proof available.[15] The answer, immediately supplied in the same place, was simply that these persons were not to be forced in any way by the Church authorities to remain as married persons, or to cohabit, even if only one of them denied the fact. Thus both the affirmation of the man and of the woman had to be given to secure the Church's approval for their continued cohabitation. A final notation proclaimed that a marriage contracted in a clandestine manner began without recognition from the Church, and gained this recognition only after its publication or approval. The acknowledgment of the

[12] C. 2, X, *de clan. desp.*, IV, 3; *Comp. I,* IV, 3, 3; JL, n. 13774.

[13] "Si matrimonio ita occulte contrahuntur, quod exinde legitima probatio non appareat, ii qui ea contrahunt, ab ecclesia non sunt aliquatenus compellendi. Verum si personae contrahentium hoc voluerint publicare, nisi rationabilis causa praepediat, ab ecclesia recipienda sunt, et comprobanda, tamquam a principio in ecclesiae conspectu contracta."—c. 2, X, *de clan. desp.*, IV, 3.

[14] *Glossa Ordinaria,* c. 2, X, *de clan. desp.*, IV, 3.

[15] C. 2, X, *de clan. desp.*, IV, 3, s.v. *Quod vobis.*

children of such a union as legitimate from the time of the secret marriage accompanied this approval.

The denial of one or both parties that the marriage took place not only removed the possibility of the Church's insisting that they remain together, but posited the necessity of their separating, since in living together they were presumed to be guilty of fornication or incest. This was the comment of Bernard of Parma.[16] He recalled a passage in Gratian according to which persons who were married were excluded from sacred orders, but the marriage in such a case had to be publicly known, if it was occult, then judgment concerning it was to be left to God.[17] Several other passages noted the refusal on the part of the Church to render judgment in secret matters,[18] still a marriage, whether public or occult, was counted invalid if it was contracted by blood relatives.[19] Regarding the impediment of consanguinity at this time, particular legislation had determined that marriage was invalid if the parties were related by blood to the fourth, fifth, or sixth degrees. Persons married after this law had been established and in contravention of it had to be separated.[20] Hostiensis, however, declared that the forbidden degree in occult cases was the fourth or a closer one,[21] since this was also the legislation in force for public marriage,[22] and no one could prohibit what the Pope had not prohibited.

The question of proving the contraction of secret marriages could become a complicated matter, since even a valid secret marriage rendered the parties more easily capable of attempting another marriage, which subsequent marriage, if celebrated publicly, had to be presumed valid as there was then no public knowledge of the first union. Hostiensis offered a solution to this problem at some length.[23]

16 *Glossa Ordinaria,* c. 2, X, *de clan. desp.,* IV, 3, s.v. *Compellendi.*

17 C. 2, D. XXXII.

18 C. 20, C. II, q. 5; c. 7, c. VI, q. 1; c. 23, C. XXXII, q. 5.

19 C. 1, C. XXXV, q. 5.

20 C. 21, C. XXXV, q. 3.

21 *Summa Aurea,* lib. IV, tit. *de clan. desp.,* s.v. *Quam poenam.*

22 Mansi, *Sacrorum Conciliorum Nova et Amplissima Collectio* (53 vols. in 59, Paris, Arnhem, Leipzig, 1901-1927), XX, 1038.

23 *Summa Aurea,* lib. IV, tit. *de clan. desp.,* s.v. *Quare prohibeantur.*

He indicated that there existed a general prohibition against secret marriages, for when one of the spouses changed his or her mind, no assurances of the fact of the secretly contracted marriage could be presented to the judge. Inasmuch as persons who had contracted secret marriages could not by any application of the law be hindered from contracting second marriages, the situation which was thus made possible could occasion the danger of many snares of conscience. On the one hand, the consciences of such persons reminded them that they were not entitled to the right of intercourse in their second, attempted marriages, since it remained invalid in view of the first marriage. On the other hand, *in foro iudiciali* they were subject to excommunication unless they rendered the marital debt whenever it was rightfully sought by the partner in their second union, who was not aware of the invalidity of this union. In practice, so continued Hostiensis, three variously deduced solutions were followed. Some persons tolerated the excommunication, since it was the opinion of theologians that they should do so, inasmuch as no one was ever permitted to act contrary to his conscience. Others, although knowing that the first consent still endured, continued living in their second marriage, once they had secured the opinion of a judge which favored its validity. They were of the opinion that sin could be excused in circumstances wherein an external demand of the law was fulfilled, thereby wrongly interpreting a canon of Gratian.[24] The third group sought the advice of canonical jurisprudence in their predicament. In this last method a reasonable solution of the problem was obtainable. The first solution Hostiensis called praiseworthy, the second bestial, and the third reasonable.

Second marriages when publicly contracted enjoyed the presumption of the law in their favor, for the preceding clandestine marriages could not be established through legitimate witnesses.[25] Therefore, unless before the second and public marriage there was submitted either a confession of the parties or some proof through witnesses regarding the fact of the first marriage, the Church authorities stood for the public marriage if there was any question which involved

[24] C. 1, C. XXIII, q. 4.

[25] *Summa Aurea*, lib. IV, tit. *de clan. desp.*, s.v. *Quot modis.*

either or both unions in the ecclesiastical courts. In the event that more than one secret marriage had been entered, it did not suffice simply to establish proof concerning one of them, for the existence of all of them had to be made manifest. If the existence of such unions was not proclaimed at the outset of the difficulty, they could not be proclaimed afterwards, except when certain proof could furthermore be supplied for the alleged marriages. This presumption in favor of the second or later marriage which was entered publicly was emphasized in another passage by the same author.[26] Even though the earlier unions may have been true and valid marriages, the inability to establish their existence by convincing proof stood in the way of enforcing any juridical consequences as deriving from such marriages. Thus a practical solution was offered as far as the application of external law was concerned. But the problem of conscience was really left untouched since *"de internis non iudicat praetor."*

Gregory IX's Decretals contained more than simple prohibitions against secret marriages. The reasons for the prohibitions were explained and the prescribed manner of publicizing a marriage was added. Gregory made use of the condemnation of clandestine marriages uttered by Innocent III (1198-1216) in the Fourth General Council of the Lateran in the year 1215.[27] Innocent recalling that the prohibition against marriages between those related by blood within the last three degrees had been abolished, demanded that this same prohibition still be observed in the other degrees. Adhering to the mind of his predecessors, he forbade clandestine marriages, and warned priests against witnessing them. He required that proposed marriages be publicly announced in Church during a fixed and suitable time. The purpose of this procedure was to make it possible for persons who knew of impediments to the marriage to make these hindrances known. Priests in arranging marriages were bound to investigate the status of the persons in order to determine whether impediments to the marriage existed. In the presence of a probable impediment the proposed union was to be expressly forbidden until

[26] Hostiensis, *Summa Aurea,* lib. IV, tit. *de clan. desp.,* s.v. *Quare prohibeantur.*

[27] C. 3, X, *de clan. desp.,* IV, 3; *Comp. IV,* IV, 2. 1.

it was evident from reliable sources what was to be done in regard to it.[28]

It is not clear to whom Innocent III referred in stating that he was invoking the prohibition of his predecessors in condemning secret marriages. The canon of Pope Evaristus is cited as indicative of at least one of his predecessors to whom he had reference.[29] However, this canon has already been discussed,[30] and it is generally conceded to be spurious.

The prohibition against clandestine marriages as pronounced by Innocent III, and as incorporated by Gregory IX in his Decretals, forbade secret marriages of three types.[31] The first was that in which there were no witnesses to the marriage, and the second was that in which the required solemnities were not included in the ceremony, as had been indicated by Gratian.[32] The third was that which abstracted from the tenor of the canon under discussion, namely, a marriage contracted without the required proclamations.

With reference to the obligation of revealing known impediments, any deliberate failure in this regard amounted to a quasi-public crime.[33] Not only could everyone, without distinction, make the denunciation, but everyone with the required knowledge was held to do so, even if he had only a probable opinion that the impediment was present. Blood relations of the contracting parties were to be given more credence in their statements than others who volunteered to give information.

Gregory IX, employing the language of Innocent III, continued in his decretal to indicate the evil effects of secret marriages. If anyone presumed to enter clandestine or interdicted marriages within the prohibited grades, even through ignorance, the offspring of such a union was to be considered absolutely illegitimate.[34] It seems at

[28] Schroeder, *Disciplinary Decrees of the General Councils: Text, Translation and Commentary,* (St. Louis: Herder, 1937), pp. 578-579 (for the Latin text), pp. 280-281 (for the English translation).

[29] *Glossa Ordinaria,* c. 3, X, *de clan. desp.,* IV, 3, s.v. *Praedecessorum.*

[30] *Supra,* p. 7.

[31] *Glossa Ordinaria,* c. 3, X, *de clan. desp.,* s.v. *Clandestina.*

[32] C. XXX, q. 5.

[33] *Glossa Ordinaria,* c. 3, X, *de clan. desp.,* s.v. *Voluerit.*

[34] C. 3, X, *de clan. desp.,* IV, 3; *Comp. IV,* IV, 2. 1.

least that there was a difference indicated between the clandestine and the interdicted marriage. Bernard of Parma († 1266), declared the clandestine marriage to be the one which was entered without publications of any kind having been made.[35] This he contraposed to the interdicted marriage, which was entered into after there was alleged a probable cause which forbade the marriage.[36]

Hostiensis († 1271) stated regarding the above mentioned illegitimacy of the children of clandestine and interdicted marriages that it affected only the children who were born before the marriage was approved by the Church.[37] If they were born after the Church's approval of the marriage, even if they were conceived before it, they were to be considered legitimate. The offspring then, of persons who married secretly, though they knew nothing of the presence of an impediment, was illegitimate. If both parties, knowing of the presence of an impediment, nevertheless presumed to enter marriage either secretly or publicly, in spite of the interdict which was placed upon their attempt to do so, the children likewise were illegitimate.[38] Relative to the question of legitimacy the law was not altogether conclusive for all possible cases, since it determined nothing for the case in which a public marriage was contracted in good faith on the part of both or only one of the parties.

The last section of the decretal as repeated from the law of Innocent III by Gregory IX determined the penalties which were to be imposed on the violators of the law. If the parish priest deliberately neglected to forbid clandestine or interdicted unions, or if any of the regular clergy presumed to witness them, he was to be suspended from office for three years, a graver punishment being in store if the nature of the offense demanded it.[39] The marriages referred to were those which were clandestine, or in which there was present an impediment, or relative to which an impediment was at least alleged.[40] Hostiensis declared that the penalty enacted for

[35] *Glossa Ordinaria*, c. 3, X, *de clan. desp.*, IV, 3, s.v. *Clandestina.*
[36] *Glossa Ordinaria*, c. 3, X, *de clan. desp.*, IV, 3, s.v. *Interdicta.*
[37] *Summa Aurea*, lib. IV, tit. *de clan. desp.*, s.v. *Quam poenam.*
[38] C. 3, X, *de clan. desp.*, IV, 3.
[39] C. 3, X, *de clan. desp.*, IV, 3.
[40] *Glossa Ordinaria*, c. 3, X, *de clan. desp.*, IV, 3, s.v. *Tales.*

parochial priests, secular or religious, was to be operative not only if the priest were actually present, but even if he simply heard that the marriage was planned and thereupon neglected to forbid it.[41] He added that if a legate of the Holy See imposed a penalty because of violations of these regulations regarding secret marriages, the Bishops of the persons involved had not the power to remit punishments reserved to the legate himself.

Persons marrying secretly, even when no impediment existed to their marriage, were to be punished with a condign and suitable penance.[42] The foundation for such a penance was the fact that such a marriage had to be regarded as one which was undertaken in contempt of the command of ecclesiastical authorities.[43] If a father forced his son or daughter into a secret marriage, then some of the decretalists held that only the father became subject to the punishment. But Hostiensis insisted that, since the essence of marriage rests in its consent, it seemed that the son or daughter also became liable to the penalty.[44]

Hostiensis drew up a summary of the four general ways in which clandestine marriages could be effected, as found in the Decree of Gratian and in the Decretal legislation of Gregory IX.[45] His words form an excellent and concise statement of most of the points that have been discussed in the two chapters preceding. For this reason they are here briefly reiterated.

1. A marriage was clandestine if the required solemnities were not observed. These solemnities included the blessing in church, the giving of the dowry, the presentation of the woman at the hands of her parents or guardian, and the prayers for chastity in marriage. If one omitted some of these solemnities, and the marriage was not clandestine in any other manner, then the sin which was committed was scarcely to be considered as grave. But if all the solemnities were completely passed over, the parties were

41 *Summa Aurea,* lib. IV, tit. *de clan. desp.,* s.v. *Quam poenam.*
42 C. 3, X, *de clan. desp.,* IV, 3.
43 C. 3, X, *de clan. desp.,* IV, 3, s.v. *Poenitentia.*
44 *Summa Aurea,* lib. IV, tit. *de clan. desp.,* s.v. *Quam poenam.*
45 *Summa Aurea,* lib. IV, tit. *de clan. desp.,* s.v. *Quot modis.*

to be considered as acting in contempt of the ecclesiastical authority, and subsequently incurred the guilt of sin if they exchanged the enjoyment of marital rights.

2. Marriage contracted secretly, and without witnesses, was definitely a clandestine union. Obviously the failure to observe ecclesiastical demands was of much more serious character in such a marriage, than in cases where the solemnities were omitted. Those who lived in unions of this type were to be perpetually excommunicated, or, in the event that either or both contracted a new marriage, the later union was branded as being adulterous in character.

3. Marriage which was entered secretly and without the permission of the Bishop was likewise a clandestine union. This case was realized when one party to a proposed marriage was already bound by a promise *de futuro* to another; the situation was, of course, much more serious, if the original promise was made in words *de praesenti.* Persons offending in this manner were to be given a severe penance. This punishment attached to those who attended the clandestine marriage as well as to the parties themselves, though in a lesser degree.

4. Lastly, that marriage was clandestine for which the banns were not announced, though no permission for their omission had been obtained from the Bishop. This classification also included those cases in which there was a concealment of any adversary who could have disclosed information militating against the celebration of the proposed marriage. To those who were guilty in these ways there was to be administered a condign penalty, which, in the case of pastors guilty of neglect, was at least a suspension of three years. Naturally it was possible that given cases of clandestinity in marriage might have contained the characteristics of more than one of the situations above described. In such instances the parties were to be punished according to their several delinquencies, and the marriage judged in the light of the accumulated defects.

Secret marriages constituted a definite and widespread problem in the Church of the Middle Ages. As has been indicated, they were always regarded unfavorably by the hierarchy. There is no place, however, in pre-Tridentine legislation wherein any authoritative statement of their invalidity can be found. The situation became even more acute with the increasing evils of clandestinity, but it was not until a definite required form for marriage was established that the elimination of the evils could be realized.

CHAPTER III

FROM THE COUNCIL OF TRENT TO THE DECREE *SATIS VOBIS*

ARTICLE I. EFFECT OF THE *Tametsi* LEGISLATION ON SECRET MARRIAGES

TILL the time of the Council of Trent (1545-1563) it had been generally acknowledged that secret marriages were valid, though illicit.[1] This previous essential validity was asserted by the Fathers of the Council themselves,[2] and it was only after lengthy and serious discussion and consideration that there was reached a decision which condemned clandestine marriages as invalid.[3] However, on November 11, 1563, the decree known as the *Tametsi* was approved. After stating the position of the Church regarding clandestinity in marriage, and her right to legislate against it, the decree proposed that in the future all marriages had to be announced publicly three times in church; they had to be celebrated in the presence of the proper pastor, or priest properly delegated, and two or three witnesses, and,

[1] Gasparri, *Tractatus Canonicus de Matrimonio* (2 vols., Parisiis, 1891), II, n. 1032; Allègre, *Impedimentorum Matrimonii Synopsis* (4. ed., Parisiis, 1889), p. 66; Dillon, *Common Law Marriage,* The Catholic University of America Canon Law Studies, n. 153, (Washington, D. C.: The Catholic University of America Press, 1942), p. 34; Donovan, *The Pastor's Obligation in Pre-nuptial Investigation,* The Catholic University of America Canon Law Studies, n. 115 (Washington, D. C.: The Catholic University of America, 1938), p. 30.

[2] Conc. Trident., sess. XXIV, *de ref. matrim.*, c. 1.

[3] This controversy is outlined in *Concilii Tridentini Diariorum, Actorum, Epistolarum Tractatum Nova Collectio,* (ed. Societas Görresiana, Friburgi, Brisgoviae: B. Herder, 1901-1938), IX, 939; Sanchez, *Tres Libri Disputationum de Sancto Matrimonii Sacramento* (Antwerpiae, 1626), lib. III, d. 4, n. 7 (Hereafter this work will be cited simply as Sanchez); Carberry, *The Juridical Form of Marriage,* pp. 20, 23. Dillon, *Common Law Marriage,* p. 35.

after the ceremony, had to be recorded in the parochial marriage register.[4]

This decree, enacted for the purpose of ensuring the publication of marriages, and of removing the dangers of clandestinity by means of invalidating the unions which were entered in disregard of the prescribed *Tametsi* form,failed to make provision for cases wherein absolute secrecy was justifiable and necessary. These cases existed when persons who had lived in concubinage but ultimately were desirous of contracting marriage were in danger of suffering great hardship or sincere detriment if their marriage was made public. Thus one of the evils previously decried as associated with clandestinity, namely, the inability of ecclesiastical authorities to properly curb concubinage was not eliminated by the Tridentine law. As a result concubinage continued to be practised, for the pre-Tridentine escape from the stigma of invalidity in marriage by means of the illicit clandestine marriage was no longer a possibility.

Pertinent especially to the future development of the Marriage of Conscience were the requirements of the announcments, of the assistance of the proper pastor, and of the registration of the marriage as decreed in the *Tametsi* legislation. With sufficient reason the Ordinary,[5] could dispense from the banns completely or allow them to be made after marriage, though before its consummation.[6] A dispensation of this kind did however not eliminate the attendant publicity, which elimination was desired for the Marriage of Conscience, and the Ordinary in granting the dispensation from the banns could hardly hope to effect the desired absolute secrecy. Marriage *praesente parocho* was also of interest from the viewpoint of the Marriage of Conscience, since in an effort to preserve secrecy many persons attempted marriage in places where they were unknown and

4 Conc. Trident., sess. XXIV, *de ref. matrim.,* c. 1.

5 The term "Ordinary" then included the Vicar General, the Vicar Capitular, *sede vacante,* and others. Cf. Mazzaeus, *De Matrimonio Conscientiae* (Romae, 1766), p. 15; Sanchez, lib. III, d. 7, c. 4; Schmalzgrueber, *Ius Ecclesiasticum Universum* (5 vols. in 12, 1843-1845) lib. IV, tit. III, n. 25; Roberts, *The Banns of Marriage,* The Catholic University of America Canon Law Studies, n. 64 (Washington, D. C.: The Catholic University of America, 1931), pp. 34, 36.

6 Conc. Trident., sess. XXIV, *de ref. matrim.,* c. 1.

had no domicile. The Holy See confirmed the teaching that the pastor whom the law postulated in the *Tametsi* was the proper pastor, that is, the pastor of the place where either party had a domicile.[7] Finally, the required recording of marriages in the regular parochial marriage register presented a serious obstacle to the sure maintenance of secrecy, for there was not offered by the Fathers of the Council any alternative which still was in keeping with the law.

Although the *Tametsi* legislation was confirmed in a Bull of Pius IV (1559-1565) as approved ecclesiastical legislation,[8] it bound only where it was promulgated in accord with the mode of promulgation which was determined by the Council itself.[9] Wherever the law of the Council of Trent did not become effective, the regulations of the IV General Council of the Lateran remained in force, together with the local laws and customs existing in that place.[10] The practical effect of the decree *Tametsi* on clandestine marriages was, therefore, that they were invalid wherever the Tridentine form bound if they were attempted in complete disregard of that form, but where this legislation did not bind, secret marriages were valid, in the ways they had been universally valid till the time of the Council of Trent, as long as they were not contracted *in fraudem legis.*

[7] Urbanus VIII, const. *Exponi nobis,* 14 aug. 1627—*Bullarii Romani Continuatio Summorum Pontificum,* (19 vols., Prato, 1756-1883), XIII, 537; Benedictus XIV, const. *Paucis abhinc,* 19 mart. 1758—*Fontes,* n. 447; Vermeersch-Creusen, *Epitome,* II, n. 382; Donovan, *The Pastor's Obligation in Pre-nuptial Investigation,* p. 31.

[8] *Benedictus Deus,* 7 febr. 1564—Schroeder, *Canons and Decrees of the Council of Trent* (St. Louis: B. Herder, 1941), p. 532.

[9] Conc. Trident., sess. XXIV, *de ref. matrim.,* c. 1; for detailed information regarding the manner of promulgation and the extent of the influence of the *Tamesti* legislation cf. Benedictus XIV, *De Synodo Dioecesana* (2 vols., Romae: Typographia S. C. de Propaganda Fide, 1806), lib. XIII, c. 5, n. 6; Zitelli-Natali, *Apparatus Iuris Ecclesiastici* (Romae: Ex typis Soc. Edit. Rom., 1886), pp. 390, 392-402; Gasparri, *De Matrimonio,* II, n. 1047; Vermeersch-Creusen, *Epitome,* II, n. 385; Allègre, *Impedimentorum Matrimonii Synopsis,* pp. 68, 70; *Acta et Decreta Concilii Plenarii Baltimorensis Tertii* (Baltimorae: John Murphy, 1886), n. 255.

[10] Benedctus XIV, const. *Paucis abhinc,* 19 mart 1758, § 3—*Fontes,* n. 447.

Article II. Secret Marriages where the *Tametsi* Was not Promulgated

In places where the *Tametsi* never came into force the validity of marriages could not be disproved simply because of their clandestinity. Simple clandestinity existed when neither pastor nor witnesses had assisted at the marriage.[11] Such unions, though valid, were always illicit, because of the command of the Church to contract marriage publicly, and because of the evils consequent upon these marriages.[12] However, authors differed in assigning the precise reasons why these unions were illicit. Sanchez (1550-1610), proposing the opinion of others,[13] stated that clandestine marriages were *ipso iure* illicit since they entailed of their very nature grave evils to the children of such marriages, to the state, and to the parties themselves. These evils, he insisted, placed clandestine marriages in a special class of marriages intrinsically evil, and all marriages of this type shared in the same illicitness. Just as lies and fornications were in all cases in trinsically wrong by their nature, so were clandestine marriages. Others denied the proposal of Sanchez, affirming that the reason for illicitness in clandestine marriages could be found in human law alone, that is, in the positive law of the Church.[14] If this last opinion were not true, then those who entered these marriages secretly would in every instance have been guilty of grave sin, in accord with the opinion of Sanchez, even when no other way of entering marriage was possible to the persons involved, so that clandestine marriages had to be regarded as permissible. The view of Schmalzgrueber (1663-1735) and Pirhing (1606-1679) appeared more reasonable and better founded, and since it represented also a common opinion it became

[11] Allègre, *Impedimentorum Matrimonii Synopsis,* p. 65.

[12] Pirhing, *Ius Canonicum Novo Methodo Explicatum* (ed. novissima, 5 vols., Dilingae, 1728) lib. IV, tit. III, n. 2; Gasparri, *De Matrimonio,* II, n. 1032.

[13] Lib. IV, disp. 3, n. 7; according to Sanchez his opinion in this place is drawn from and supported by Cajetan, Veracruz, Matienzo, and Ledesma.

[14] Schmalzgrueber, lib. IV, tit. III, n. 93; Pirhing, lib. IV, tit. III, n. 4.

the one more generally followed by later authors.[15]

The old problem of deciding upon whom rested the obligation of proving a strictly secret marriage,[16] was settled. When none but the contracting parties knew of the existence of a marriage, the fact of marriage was to be admitted by a judge on the positive assertion of both parties, or it was to be regarded as non-existent if both persons involved denied it. If one alleged that a valid marriage had taken place, and the other denied it, the burden of proof remained with the party asserting the fact of marriage.[17] In this manner the unexplained assertion in the Decretals of Gregory IX was disposed of.[18]

It is not possible to give here a detailed history of the development of the secret marriage in places where the *Tametsi* did not bind. The marriage legislation in force before the Council of Trent in the whole world continued unchanged in the places not affected by the *Tametsi,* with the few changes noted above. No outstanding change occurred to alter the status of these marriages till the decree *Ne temere* began to bind on April 19, 1908.[19] This decree made the ecclesiastical form of marriage a requirement for validity in all marriages in which at least one party was a Latin Catholic. From that time on a simple neglect of the prescribed form resulted in an invalid marriage, whether secret or public.

15 Gasparri, *De Matrimonio,* II, n. 1032, footnote 1; Wernz, *Ius Decretalium* (6 vols., Romae, Prati, 1898-1905, [Vol. IV, *Ius Matrimoniale,* 1904], IV, n. 158, note 92.

16 *Supra,* pp. 14-16.

17 Gonzalez-Tellez, *Commentaria Perpetua In Singulos Textus Quinque Librorum Decretalium Gregorii IX* (5 vols., Venetiis, 1699), lib. IV, tit. III, c. 4; Santi, *Praelectiones Iuris Canonici* (2. ed., 5 vols., Ratisbonae: F. Pustet, 1892), lib. IV, tit. III, n. 33; Gasparri, *De Matrimonio,* II, n. 1938.

18 *Supra,* p. 14.

19 S. C. C., decr., 2 aug. 1907—*Fontes,* n. 4340 *Acta Sanctae Sedis* (41 vols., Romae, 1865-1908), XL (1908), 527.

Article III. Development of the Marriage of Conscience Before the *Satis Vobis*

A. No Express Legislation in the Council of Trent

There were no definite norms given by the Church authorities before the Constitution *Satis Vobis* in 1741 [20] providing for Marriages of Conscience in the external forum.[21] Secrecy, in the legislation of the Council of Trent, could exist in two cases, namely when a dispensation from the banns had been obtained and valid marriage ensued, or when an invalid union was effected without the proper priest and witnesses being present.[22] There was an opinion that this last type of purely clandestine invalid marriage constituted a Marriage of Conscience, even where the *Tametsi* was promulgated.[23] But this inaccuracy was explained to indicate the use of a given term to include all secret marriages, whether valid or not. The need for norms pointing out the procedure to be followed when strict secrecy was required in marriage was not felt in Italy, nor were Marriages of Conscience prevalent in that country.[24] None the less the need for some direction was apparent to Prosper Cardinal de Lambertinis, who as Secretary of the Congregation of the Council formulated answers to doubts and gave counsel on questions concerned with secret marriages. The responses of the Congregation of the Council and the additional notes of Cardinal de Lambertinis, who later as Benedict XIV instituted the Marriage of Conscience,[25]

[20] Benedictus XIV, ep. encycl., 17 nov. 1741—*Fontes,* n. 319.

[21] Mazzaeus, *De Matrimonio Conscientiae,* p. 153.

[22] Sess., XXIV, *de ref. matrim.,* c. 1; Reiffenstuel, *Ius Canonicum Universum* (4 vols., Venetiis, 1735), lib. IV, tit. III, n. 1.

[23] Pallottini, *Collectio Omnium Conclusionum et Resolutionum Quae in Causis Propositis apud Sacram Congregationem Cardinalium S. Concilii Tridentini Interpretum Prodierunt ab ejus institutione anno MDLIV ad annum MDCCCLX, distinctis titulis alphabetico ordine per materias digesta* (17 vols., Romae, 1868-1893), "Matrimonium," § XXVI, n. 4. (Hereafter this work will be cited simply as Pallottini).

[24] Andreucci, *Hierarchia Ecclesiastica in Varias Suas Partes Distributa* (2 vols., Romae: Generosus Salomonus, 1766), II, 62.

[25] Ep. Encycl. *Satis Vobis,* 17 nov. 1741—*Fontes,* n. 319; Pallottini, "Matrimonium", § XXVI, n. 3.

serve to indicate the attitude of the Church toward Marriages of Conscience, and display the developments made in dealing with these marriages for the time between the Council of Trent and the Constitution *Satis Vobis*. The points discussed in these responses were principally concerned with determining the substance of a valid Marriage of Conscience, with deciding who could permit and record them, and with fixing the procedure to be followed.

B. Some Invalid Unions Called Marriages of Conscience

Without doubt there were several types of marriage called Marriages of Conscience which were simply invalid forms of marriage. Some had recommended Marriages of Conscience for those in Sacred Orders as a means of avoiding incontinence, so that they could still receive the fruits of an ecclesiastical benefice, as long as the marriage remained secret.[26] But such unions were of course, simply invalid, as is evident from the decrees of the same Council which established the required form for marriage.[27]

Another union sometimes designated as a Marriage of Conscience existed in the case wherein a man and a woman, having exchanged consent privately, consummated their union with the intention of being married in the required manner when a dispensation could be obtained, or when some condition was fulfilled.[28] This attempted marriage was likewise invalid, since the form necessary for a valid marriage was not observed.[29]

A rather novel arrangement, called by some a form of the Marriage of Conscience, existed in cases in which after a dispensation from the banns was obtained and the priest was designated to assist at the marriage, the parties contracted marriage by using procurators and witnesses unknown to one another and to the pastor. The purpose of this was to ensure freedom for remarriage if the parties so desired, in which instance the children of such a marriage were classified as illegitimate as long as the first marriage remained obscured.

26 Pallottini, "Matrimonium", § XXVI, n. 4.
27 Conc. Trident., sess. XXIV, *de matrimonio,* can. 9.
28 Pallottini, "Matrimonium," § XXVI, n. 4.
29 Conc. Trident., sess. XXIV, *de ref. matrim.,* c. I.

These unions were usually valid, but the parties to them were in a state of serious sin till the circumstances which attended the contraction of marriage were rectified.[30]

These three types of unions, designated in some instances as Marriages of Conscience, were either ordinary invalid marriages, or marriages entered in a sinful and disapproved fashion. Therefore, they cannot rightly be grouped with Marriages of Conscience contracted under the direction of competent ecclesiastical authorities.

C. *Valid Marriages of Conscience*

1. DIFFERENT TYPES EVOLVED IN THE DEVELOPMENT

Not all types of Marriage of Conscience were illegal, even in this early period. During the seventeenth century it became the practice, in cases wherein it was necessary to avoid scandal, to secure a dispensation from the banns, granted by the Major Cardinal Penitentiary, with the attached faculty of having the pastor of the parties perform the marriage with two witnesses. Strict secrecy was to be observed, and the case was usually one in which the parties had really been living in concubinage, though they were believed by public repute to be married. The word *Laceratis* was written on the document granting the faculties in order to indicate that once the marriage was performed the letter of this Tribunal was to be torn up, and no record of the marriage was to be made in the parochial marriage register.[31]

There is no doubt that this type of Marriage of Conscience was valid, but the possible evils resulting from it were likewise evident. If the pastor who had performed the marriage had died there no longer remained for a marriage of this kind any way for proving the fact of the marriage, or for safeguarding the reputation of the children. One new pastor when confronted with such a case, and unable to prove the marriage in question by documentary proof, but having found that the witnesses were still alive, advised the parties who alleged their marriage to renew their consent before himself

30 Pallottini, "Matrimonium", § XXVI, n. 4.

31 Pallottini, *loc. cit.*

and the two original witnesses.[32] However, both parties were ready to swear that they had been joined validly in a Marriage of Conscience previously, and then there was proposed to the Congregation of the Council the question whether these persons could renew their consent without admitting that they had been guilty of serious sin. The response was negative, and the procedure to be followed was indicated.[33] The recommendation written by Cardinal Altovito, then Secretary of the Congregation, stated the duty of the pastor to receive orally the testimonies of the witnesses and of the parties to the alleged marriage, and, when he had been shown a duplicate of the original document sent by the Sacred Penitentiary when that Tribunal permitted the marriage, to record the fact of marriage in the marriage register. This, Pallottini observes, seemed somewhat ill advised, since in an authentic document received from the Sacred Penitentiary there would not have appeared either the names of the parties, or of the pastor.[34]

For the purpose of avoiding difficulties in cases similar to the one just described, the practice later developed in the Sacred Penitentiary of granting, on the petition of the couple living in concubinage, the faculty for them to marry before their proper pastor and two trustworthy witnesses apart from the making of any previous announcements. Each such permission included a positive command to record the marriage in a book, and omitted the clause *Laceratis*. In the event of an occult impediment being present, a twofold concession was necessary from the Sacred Penitentiary. One rescript was to be directed to a confessor to dispense from the impediment, and in this document the clause *Laceratis* was included; a second rescript was to be sent to the pastor of the parties to be used after the dispensation from the impediment had been executed, and then was not to be destroyed. The marriage was to be recorded in a book. If a priest other than the pastor was granted these faculties, he was obliged to note the fact of the marriage, and of his having delegation to witness it, in the parochial marriage register.[35]

[32] Pallottini, "Matrimonium", § XXVI, n. 5.
[33] Resp., 19 sept. 1684—Pallottini, "Matrimonium", § XXVI, n. 5.
[34] Pallottini, "Matrimonium", § XXVI, n. 5.
[35] Pallottini, "Matrimonium", § XXVI, n. 5.

It is interesting to observe that the pastor was to record the marriage in "a book," but the delegated priest in "the parochial marriage register." The book which was to be used by the pastor appears to have been different from the parochial marriage register and in this can possibly be found the beginning of the completely separate registration of secret marriages in a marriage register distinct from the one used for the recording of other marriages. It is certain that the procedure of using a different book or document to record Marriages of Conscience was developed some time before the requirement placed in the *Satis Vobis* in 1741,[36] though such a view is at variance with the impression conveyed by recent authors that secret and separate registration of Marriages of Conscience does not antedate the *Satis Vobis*.[37]

The most favored form of procedure was that which was followed in Rome itself. The usual dispensation from the banns, and designation of the pastor, or other priest, was obtained from the Bishop. The priest so designated was to witness the marriage, having secured two trustworthy witnesses. Causes for seeking this permission were the widely differing circumstances of the parties desiring to marry, their existing secret concubinage, or, in some cases, the bitter opposition of parents or relatives to a marriage otherwise advisable. When such a marriage had taken place, it was to be registered in the usual marriage book, but the section of this book used for recording these marriages was to bear the seal of the Bishop, and its secret information was in no case to be revealed without the permission of the Bishop. If the Bishop so desired he could require that no record of these secret marriages be kept among the parish records, but rather that records of such marriages be sent to the Bishop to be preserved with the Acts of the Episcopal Curia and Matrimonial Secrets.[38] Later the practice was recommended of

[36] Pallottini, "Matrimonium", § XXVI, n. 3.

[37] Louis, *Diocesan Archives,* The Catholic University of America Canon Law Studies, n. 137 (Washington, D. C.: The Catholic University of America Press, 1941), p. 20; O'Rourke, *Parish Registers,* The Catholic University of America Canon Law Studies, n. 88 (Washington, D. C.: The Catholic University of America, 1934), p. 38.

[38] Pallottini, "Matrimonium", § XXVI, n. 6.

noting the fact of marriage on the document giving permission for its celebration, which document, with the notation, was to be returned within three days of the celebration of the marriage to the Bishop, to be retained among the Matrimonial Secrets of the Diocese.[39]

This last species of Marriage of Conscience was valid and licit, since it was in keeping with the procedure most approved, and the one followed in Rome itself. The same regulations were to be followed in arranging the marriage of a nobleman who upon the death of his first wife, a noblewoman, desired marriage to avoid incontinence, but did not wish to dissipate his children's inheritance, or to harm their social standing, in consequence of a public second marriage with a woman of inferior rank. Marriages of this type were known as morganatic, from a Saxon word indicating the gift a husband gave his wife on the morning after the marriage.[40] The man agreed to support this second wife and whatever children she might have. Marriage of this type carried out in secrecy were justifiable,[41] and occur even today as morganatic Marriages of Conscience.[42]

2. THE QUESTION OF SCANDAL

In some instances a problem of scandal arose when persons who had really contracted a Marriage of Conscience were reputed, in the public eye, to be living in concubinage with no ecclesiastical recrimination. Theophylus Reynaud (✝ 1663) is quoted as saying that by the command of Christ, everyone is forbidden to offer another direct scandal, but that indirect scandal is justifiable in cases wherein, with an excusing cause, one's action, word, or example is

39 Pallottini, "Matrimonium", § XXVI, n. 3.

40 Du Cange, *Glossarium ad Scriptores Mediae et Infimae Latinitatis* (6 vols., Paris, 1733), II, s. v. *Morganegiba.*

41 Schmalzgrueber, lib. IV, tit. I, n. 237.

42 Noldin-Schmitt, *Summa Theologia Moralis* (3 vols., Vol. I, 25. ed., 1937, Vols., II, III, 24, ed., 1936, Oeniponte: Typis et Sumptibus F. Rauch), III, n. 513; Vermeersch, *Theologia Moralis,* III, n. 687; Merkelbach, *Summa Theologia Moralis* (2. ed., 3 vols., Paris: Typis Desclée de Brouwer et Soc., 1936), II, n. 749.

merely the occasion of another's receiving scandal.[43] This opinion was applied to Marriages of Conscience wherein scandal, if it was present, was regarded not as being actively given, but rather as being passively received.

3. LICITNESS OF THESE MARRIAGES

Marriages of Conscience performed by the proper pastor or properly delegated priest before two witnesses, with the dispensation from the banns having been secured, and the notation of the marriage having been made in the parish marriage book, were both valid and licit it seems. Certainly they were valid, even when no dispensation from the banns had been obtained, since failure to seek this dispensation in cases wherein the announcements were to be omitted did not affect the validity of the marriage.[44] These marriages were also defended as licit, since for a just cause a dispensation from the banns could be granted, and there appear to have been justifying causes present when the dispensation was granted.[45] In fact, there was an opinion that, if the pastor used due diligence to discover that no impediment existed, and then proceeded to assist at the marriage even without seeking a dispensation, his action was at most venially sinful.[46]

On the other hand, the power to dispense from the banns was possessed not only by the Bishop, but by other Ordinaries as well, including the Vicar General, the Vicar Capitular, and Abbots having quasi-judicial jurisdiction, unless this was denied to them.[47] However, this faculty was conceded in the Council of Trent [48] to be used for public marriage, and not one which was accomplished in complete secrecy. Moreover, in a Marriage of Conscience a dispensation from the recording of the marriage was required, which the

43 Pallottini, "Matrimonium", § XXVI, n. 8.

44 Gonzalez-Tellez, lib. IV, tit. III, n. 14; Pirhing, lib. IV, tit. III, n. 27; Sanchez, lib. IV, disp. 3, n. 3; Pallottini, "Matrimonium", § XXXVI, n. 7.

45 Pallottini, *loc. cit.*

46 Sanchez, lib. III, disp. 5, n. 5.

47 Reiffenstuel, lib. IV, tit. III, n. 34; Sanchez, lib. III, disp. 7, n. 4.

48 Sess., XXIV, *de ref. matrim.*, c. 1.

Bishop could not give on his own authority.[49]

Again, even if the Bishop's powers to dispense from the banns included use of this power in granting permission for Marriages of Conscience, the logical conclusion was that the Vicar General, the Vicar Capitular, and the Abbots could likewise dispense in this manner. Since several of these superiors often exercised their powers within the same territory, the resultant confusion and inadvisability of such a procedure is obvious. Regarding cases for which no notation or record of the marriage was made at all, such an omission would certainly not have affected the validity of the marriage.[50] According to some, failure to record the marriage together with the omission of the banns in no way affected either the validity or the licitness of a Marriage of Conscience, since banns and registration pertained only to the solemnity of marriage, and did not detract in any way from the substance of this Sacrament.[51] Nor did these omissions imply that proofs were entirely lacking, since registration was not considered an essential condition for proving the marriage.[52]

Because of the absence of definite legislation treating of Marriages of Conscience between the date of the Council of Trent and that of the Constitution *Satis Vobis,* no exact detailed conclusions can be drawn for this period, though a progressive development of this canonical institute is discernible. Abstracting from the obviously invalid cases, these marriages were generally valid and licit, if they were contracted with sufficient reason, and if the approved instructions of ecclesiastical superiors were followed. Their licitness depended on the circumstances in each case, as did the advisability of exhibiting the record of such marriages when requested. This was the attitude of the Sacred Congregation of the Council in 1724 in supplying direction to those inquiring about the licitness of Marriages of Conscience, the need of registering them, and the obligation to reveal them when the circumstances demanded it.[53]

49 Mazzaeus, *De Matrimonio Conscientiae,* p. 15.

50 Sanchez, lib. III, disp. 15, n. 22.

51 Pallottini, "Matrimonium", § XXVI, n. 8.

52 This view was put forth in a decision of the Sacred Roman Rota, July 21, 1611.—Pallottini, "Matrimonium", § XXVI, n. 10.

53 Pallottini, "Matrimonium", § XXVI, n. 8.

CHAPTER IV

FROM THE CONSTITUTION *SATIS VOBIS* TO THE CODE

ARTICLE I. PURPOSE OF THE *Satis Vobis* AND ITS GENERAL CHARACTER

IN the second year of his Pontificate, on November 17, 1741, Benedict XIV issued his Encyclical *Satis Vobis,* which had as its purpose the instruction of Bishops in the manner of arranging and solving doubts concerning Marriages of Conscience.[1] The procedure indicated in this encyclical for the external forum was also to be followed in the internal forum by the Office of the Apostolic Penitentiary in handling marriages of this kind which fell within its competence in accordance with the Constitution *Pastor Bonus* of the same Pope, in which document were defined the faculties of the Major Penitentiary, and of the Office of the Penitentiary in general.[2]

The many evils attendant upon secret or improperly contracted Marriages of Conscience were outlined in the opening paragraphs of the *Satis Vobis.*[3] These evils included the scandal arising from secret marriages believed to be concubinal unions, the dangers to the inheritance, morals, and legitimacy of the children, the possibility of the contraction of invalidly attempted second marriages after valid but secret first marriages, or, in the event that the secret marriage as an initial valid union proved unsatisfactory to the parties, their subsequent refuge in immoral unions, and finally the wrongful possession of ecclesiastical benefices by married clerics in minor orders.

One of the essential purposes of the Encyclical was to supply

[1] *Fontes,* n. 319; Benedictus XIV, *De Synodo Dioecesana* (2 vols., Romae: Typographia S. C. de Propaganda Fide, 1806), lib. XIII, c. 23, n. 12; Pallottini, "Matrimonium", § XXVI, n. 9.

[2] 13 aprilis 1744—*Bullarium SSmi Domini Nostri Benedicti Papae XIV* (4. ed., 4 vols., Venetiis, 1778), I, n. 95.

[3] Benedictus XIV, ep. encycl., 17 nov. 1741, § 1-4—*Fontes,* n. 319.

a valid and licit remedy for these evils. This was accomplished by establishing externally the Marriage of Conscience as an approved canonical institute. Such a marriage was to be allowed by the competent superior,[4] who could grant permission only after investigation and upon the presentation of a sufficiently grave reason.[5] This marriage was to be contracted in secrecy,[6] without the announcements having been made, and with the proposed manner of registration adhered to.[7] Special guarantees were to be given regarding the baptism of the offspring of such a marriage,[8] and penalties were in store for those who violated these guarantees.[9]

Before embarking on a more detailed explanation of these requisites and conditions, one must make some distinction between the Marriage of Conscience and the morganatic marriage, as they existed at the time of the promulgation of the *Satis Vobis*. Franciscus Mazzaeus, who, after 1741, was probably the first to write a work exclusively devoted to the Marriage of Conscience, insisted that this type of marriage differed from the morganatic marriage,[10] and he took exception to a contemporary who placed the two in the same class.[11] Mazzaeus determined that the basis for the distinction was discovered in the facts that in a Marriage of Conscience strict secrecy was essential, the children freely succeeded to their inheritance, and either party could be of inferior condition, while in a morganatic marriage secrecy was not always required, the succession of the children was definitely limited, and the wife was always the party in the inferior position. What value these distinctions may have had is not certain. However, consideration of the opinion of Schmalzgrueber helps greatly in achieving a clear concept of the differences which were evidenced between these two types of marriages. He declared the Marriage of Conscience and the morganatic marriage

[4] Benedictus XIV, ep. encycl. *Satis Vobis*, 17 nov. 1741, § 7—*Fontes*, n. 319.

[5] *Ibid*, § 5-6—*Fontes*, n. 319.

[6] *Ibid.* § 6—*Fontes*, n. 319.

[7] *Ibid.* § 10—*Fontes*, n. 319.

[8] *Ibid.* § 11—*Fontes*, n. 319.

[9] *Ibid.* § 12, 13—*Fontes*, n. 319.

[10] *De Matrimonio Conscientiae*, p. 8.

[11] Andreucci, *Hierarchia Ecclesiastica*, II, 62.

were originally simply divergent forms of the strictly secret marriage, therefore though essentially and in origin identical, they acquired individuating characteristics in their progress through the centuries.[12] None the less, though these two types of marriage were obviously not generically distinct, it would be of advantage to keep in mind that the morganatic marriage, except for the note of secrecy, was of stricter character, especially in the sense of being permitted by the Church in fewer cases, than the Marriage of Conscience.

Article II. Definite Provisions of This Decree

A. Cause and Investigation Required

A legitimate or serious cause sufficed for the granting of a dispensation from the banns,[13] but the granting of a dispensation was not dependent on the will of the one dispensing alone; it postulated the presence of a true cause.[14] Likewise, before he conceded permission for a Marriage of Conscience the superior was required to determine that a cause was existent, and that it constituted a grave and most urgent reason for the granting of the permission.[15] Such a cause, the encyclical continued, had been considered by the Office of the Sacred Penitentiary to exist in cases wherein the parties who were quite generally thought to be married were really living in concubinage. The mention of this specific case in the encyclical, however, was not meant to restrict the powers of the superiors for use in this one set of circumstances. It was suggested that other equally or more serious reasons might exist to justify superiors in exercising their powers.

Another cause which had been considered among the later decretalists as sufficiently grave to permit secrecy in the celebration of marriage was the completely disparate condition of the parties, espe-

12 Lib. IV, tit. I, n. 237.

13 Benedictus XIV, ep. encycl. *Nimiam Licentiam,* 18 maii 1743—*Fontes,* n. 337; Roberts, *The Banns of Marriage,* p. 38.

14 Benedictus XIV, ep. encycl. *Satis Vobis,* 17 nov. 1741, § 5—*Fontes,* n. 319; Sanchez, lib. III, disp. 8, n. 4; Schmalzgrueber, lib. III, tit. III, n. 25.

15 Benedictus XIV, ep. encycl. *Satis Vobis,* 17 nov. 1741, § 6—*Fontes,* n. 319.

cially when the marriage tended to the spiritual good of those involved.[16] This reason was recognized as grave and most urgent.[17] But if it was used as a cause for the permission which was to be granted it had to be certainly founded on the widely differing conditions of the parties, for if one party was of the middle class of society and the other of a humble station in life then the permission to contract a Marriage of Conscience was to be denied.[18] Again, the inequality required was one which had to relate to birth and position, and not merely to age. A man advanced in years could not propose the fact of his senility as a reason for seeking secret marriage with a young girl.[19] Mazzaeus remarked that in his time in places where a widow lost the guardianship of her children through remarriage, as in France, such a fact together with the attendant danger of incontinence was considered a grave enough reason for the seeking of permission in order to enter a strictly secret marriage.[20]

An injunction was laid on those who granted permissions for Marriages of Conscience to investigate not only the seriousness of the cause, but to determine whether the parties were capable of entering a valid marriage. The character, qualities, and condition of the applicants were to be diligently inquired into. If parents were opposed to the marriage, their opinion was to be considered for the sake of determining whether the celebration of the marriage was nevertheless justified. The absence of all impediments was to be made manifest, and documentary or sworn evidence of the free state of the parties was required before permission could lawfully be granted.[21]

B. Who Could Grant Permission

Those empowered to allow the external celebration of Marriages

[16] Reiffenstuel, lib. IV, tit. III, n. 1; Schmalzgrueber, lib. IV, tit. III, n. 47.

[17] Benedictus XIV, *De Synodo Dioecesana,* lib. XIII, c. 23, n. 12; Mazzaeus, *De Matrimonio Conscientiae,* p. 58.

[18] Benedictus XIV, *loc. cit.;* Mazzaeus, *op. cit.* p. 44.

[19] Mazzaeus, *op. cit.* p. 45.

[20] *Op. cit.,* p. 44.

[21] Benedictus XIV, ep. encycl. *Satis Vobis,* 17 nov. 1741, § 7—*Fontes,* n. 319.

of Conscience on the condition of the observance of strict secrecy were, other than the Pope himself, all Patriarchs, Primates, Archbishops, and Bishops, in their own territory.[22] This power generally was considered to have been possessed also by the Vicar General and the Vicar Capitular, *sede vacante,* since they were Ordinaries.[23] After the publication of the *Satis Vobis,* however, it was desired that the Bishops reserve the use of this power to themselves.[24]

The priest designated to witness the Marriage of Conscience was ordinarily to be pastor of either or both of the parties to the marriage. Naturally the pastor could be expected to have the fuller knowledge, experience, and facility required for the proper handling of these cases. Still, for a grave reason a priest other than the pastor could be designated.[25] Such a grave reason was recognized to be present when the so designated extraneous priest had a special worthiness or learning to recommend him. If, without a just cause, a Bishop selected a priest other than one of the pastors of the parties, the pastor who should have been designated, if he in some manner learned of the marriage, could appeal to the Metropolitan, in which case the Bishop could be forced to reveal his reason for selecting a priest other than one of the pastors.[26]

Likewise, if persons were refused permission by their own Bishop they could seek the permission of the Metropolitan.[27] This expedient was probably used with some degree of frequency, since Benedict XIV himself stated that permission for these marriages was not a thing altogether unusual, inasmuch as there occurred repeatedly cases in which Marriages of Conscience were to be allowed.[28]

[22] Benedictus XIV, ep. encycl. *Satis Vobis,* 17 nov. 1741—*Fontes,* n. 319.

[23] Mazzaeus, *De Matrimonio Conscientiae,* p. 15.

[24] Mazzaeus, *op. cit.* p. 19.

[25] Benedictus XIV, ep. encycl. *Satis Vobis,* 17 nov. 1741, § 8—*Fontes,* n. 319.

[26] Mazzaeus, *De Matrimonio Conscientiae,* p. 70.

[27] Mazzaeus, *op. cit.* p. 60.

[28] *De Synodo Dioecesana,* lib. XIII, c. 23, n. 13.

C. *Manner of Celebration*

1. SECRECY

With the preliminary investigation accomplished, and the cause for seeking the permission for a Marriage of Conscience having been adjudged, the priest designated was to proceed with the celebration of the marriage, observing closely the peculiar regulations given for these cases. Not only did the permission provide for the omission of the banns, but the marriage was to take place secretly, and thereupon was to be registered in a special book.[29] No express promise or oath to keep the fact of marriage a secret was prescribed in the *Satis Vobis,* but it was understood that the marriage was to be held in secrecy by the superior who granted the permission, and by the priest who was designated to witness it, and by the parties themselves and the witnesses who assisted at the marriage.[30] There was expressly proposed only one case in which the superior could take it upon himself to divulge the marriage. It was the case in which questions concerning the baptism and the legitimate status of the children were involved.[31] Therefore, the simple fact of scandal having arisen did not furnish sufficient grounds for declaring that the reason for secrecy had automatically ceased, as some said,[32] for in these cases the scandal was rather received, but not given,[33] and therefore remained an indirect effect of the marriage. Again, in a letter to Cardinal Malvezzi, Benedict XIV denied persistently that the ecclesiastical superior was obliged always to manifest a secret marriage whenever his silence implied possible injury to a third party.[34]

[29] Benedictus XIV, ep. encycl. *Satis Vobis,* 17 nov. 1741, § 6, 10—*Fontes,* n. 319.

[30] Benedictus XIV, *De Synodo Dioecesana,* lib. XIII, c. 25, n. 12.

[31] Benedictus XIV, ep. encycl. *Satis Vobis,* 17 nov. 1741, § 12—*Fontes,* n. 319.

[32] Giraldi, *Expositio Iuris Pontificii Iuxta Recentiorem Ecclesiae Disciplinam* (nova editio Romana accuratior, Romae, 1830), pars I, sectio 674, c. 2; Santi, lib. IV, tit. III, n. 33.

[33] Mazzaeus, *De Matrimonio Conscientiae,* p. 64.

[34] This letter is quoted in Mazzaeus, *op. cit.,* p. 85.

2. REGISTRATION OF THE MARRIAGE

After the celebration of a Marriage of Conscience a record of it was to be sent without delay by the witnessing priest to the Bishop. In addition to the names of the parties and the priest there were to be included indications of the time and the place, and a recording of the names of the witnesses. This record was to be transcribed exactly in a book which was used only for the purpose of registering such marriages. The pages of this book were to be joined together firmly in the fashion of a closed volume. It was to have the seal of the Bishop affixed to it and was to be guarded closely. Only the necessity of making another entry or the proper administration of justice in the case served as an excuse for opening the book a second time. The attestations themselves regarding the secretly celebrated marriage from which the recording was made, were to be sedulously preserved in an even more secret place, well constructed and secure on all sides.[35]

There was a serious obligation to follow this form of registration; however, if it was neglected, it did not affect the valid character of the marriage. An interesting case presented to the Tribunal of the Archdiocese of Salerno stands in proof of this view. Maria married John publicly on May 4, 1826. Within a year of the marriage Maria left John and returned to Vincent, by whom she had had a child previously to her marriage with John. Maria asserted that she and Vincent were married in 1824 before Thomas, pastor of both of them, and two witnesses. This marriage was performed secretly, and there was no record of it whatsoever. Thomas testified that he had witnessed both Maria's marriages, the secret one in 1824, and the public one in 1826. Both witnesses swore to the fact of the first marriage, and the presence of Thomas at the ceremony. On April 2, 1840, the Curia of Salerno decided in favor of the validity of the first marriage, that between Maria and Vincent, and the consequent invalidity of the second marriage between Maria and John.[36] This decision was proposed in the form of a doubt to the Sacred

[35] Benedictus XIV, ep. encycl. *Satis Vobis,* 17 nov. 1741, § 10—*Fontes,* n. 319.

[36] Pallottini, "Matrimonium", § XXVI, n. 12.

Congregation of the Council, which ultimately upheld the decision of the Salerno Tribunal.[37] Therefore, the failure to register secret marriages certainly did not affect their validity. None the less this decision in no way detracted from the credence which was to be given not only to the records contained in the secret marriage register, but likewise to those in the secret baptismal book, of which something will be said immediately. Both books had a probative value equal to the corresponding ordinary parochial books for which they were a substitute.[38]

D. *Provisions Concerning Children*

The priest witnessing a Marriage of Conscience was to warn the parties beforehand of their duty to educate their children in piety and good morals, allowing them to enjoy temporal goods as their means would permit.[39] The children of these marriages were to be baptized in Church, as other children were, without discrimination. Because of the secret nature of the marriage these baptisms could be performed with the names of the parents remaining secret. However, there was a strict command that the father, or in the event of his death, the mother, within thirty days, inform the Bishop of the birth and baptism of each child.[40]

This information was to come immediately from the parents personally, or in letters written by them. In some instances it was permissible to employ a trustworthy person to communicate this knowledge, for example, the priest who witnessed the ceremony. When the notification of the legitimate birth and baptism of a child was received it was to be transcribed immediately in a special baptismal register, with the correct names of the parents, by a notary

[37] *In causa Salernitana Matrimonii,* 6 mart. 1847—*Thesaurus Resolutionum Sacrae Congregationis Concilii* (167 vols., Romae, 1718-1908), CVII, 105.

[38] Benedictus XIV, ep. encycl. *Satis Vobis,* 17 nov. 1741, § 14—*Fontes,* n. 319.

[39] Benedictus XIV, ep. encycl. *Satis Vobis,* 17 nov. 1741, § 9—*Fontes,* n. 319; Benedictus XIV, *De Synodo Dioecesana,* lib. XIII, c. 23, n. 13.

[40] Benedictus XIV, ep. encycl. *Satis Vobis,* 17 nov. 1741, § 13—*Fontes,* n. 319.

or other cleric to whom had been entrusted the duty of entering all information regarding Marriages of Conscience in the proper places. The baptismal book, though separate from the book used for registering secret marriages, was to be guarded with the same diligence.[41]

Through a subsequent Marriage of Conscience children could be legitimized in the same manner as through a subsequent public marriage of their natural parents. This had always been true of secret marriage when proof of its celebration was available.[42] Before a Marriage of Conscience, therefore, it was necessary to admonish the parties of their obligations toward whatever offspring might be born of the marriage, and afterwards it was their duty to see to it that they fulfilled their offices in these respects. In fact, these Marriages were called "of Conscience" to indicate that the parties were continually to keep in mind their obligations towards one another and towards their children.[43]

E. Penalties for Non-observance of the Law

Realizing that many, prompted by human respect, would hesitate to fulfill the requirements regarding the children as agreed to before the marriage, the encyclical provided that the neglectful and contumacious were to be punished in proportion to their culpability. If a child was born and baptized, with the names of the parents being suppressed, this information was to be in the hands of the Bishop within thirty days of the birth and baptism of the child, or the fact of marriage was to be divulged.[44] The marriage was also to be revealed if some grave danger threatened the children, as some

[41] Benedictus XIV, ep. encycl. *Satis Vobis,* 17 nov. 1741, § 11—*Fontes,* n. 319; Mazzaeus, *De Matrimonio Conscientiae,* p. 97.

[42] Pirhing, lib. IV, tit. XVII, n. 36; Schmalzgrueber, lib. IV, tit. XVII, n. 53.

[43] Benedictus XIV, *De Synodo Diocesana,* lib. XIII, c. 23, n. 13; Andreucci, *Hierarchia Ecclesiastica,* II, 62; Mazzaeus, *De Matrimonio Conscientiae,* p. 9.

[44] Benedictus XIV, ep. encycl. *Satis Vobis,* 17 nov. 1741, § 12—*Fontes,* n. 319.

serious loss.[45] Mazzaeus believed that judicial action could be taken to punish one unlawfully revealing the marriage.[46]

Article III. Developments to the Present

The Encyclical *Satis Vobis* remained in force as the principal document indicating the necessary procedure and requirements in arranging Marriages of Conscience till the promulgation of the present Code of Canon Law. Over the almost two hundred intervening years the legislation of Benedict XIV pertinent to Marriages of Conscience found application in new circumstances. Its use, for example, was recommended by Leo XIII as a simple manner of circumventing unjust laws in Italy, which were fostered by the Free Masons. Laws had been enacted which demanded in every case that a civil marriage take place before any other, it being left to the discretion of the parties in each instance to decide whether they wished any other ceremony to follow. Again the state had reserved to itself the granting of permission for marriage to certain classes of people. Leo XIII, wisely realizing how these insidious rulings would encourage concubinage and foster disregard for the Sacrament of Marriage, which was no doubt what the Masons sought to accomplish, directed that when particular cases demanded it Marriages of Conscience were to be allowed.[47] The regulations of Benedict XIV were explicitly commanded to be sedulously followed and thus they continued to find application under the new circumstances as well as the old.

[45] Benedictus XIV, *De Synodo Dioecesana,* lib. XIII, c. 23, n. 13; Andreucci, *Hierarchia Ecclesiastica,* II, 62; Mazzaeus, *De Matrimonio Conscientiae,* p. 88.

[46] *Op. cit.* p. 91.

[47] Litt. *Il divisamento,* 8 febr. 1893—*Fontes,* n. 617; *Acta Sanctae Sedis* (41 vols., Romae, 1865-1908), XXV (1892-1893), 459.

CANONICAL COMMENTARY

CHAPTER V

CHARACTER OF THE MARRIAGE OF CONSCIENCE IN THE PRESENT LEGISLATION

Article I. Concept of the Marriage of Conscience

The Marriage of Conscience appears in the Code of Canon Law as a canonical institute developed over the course of centuries, which has become definite in its requirements, but which maintains sufficient flexibility to be of use in the present as well as the former circumstances requiring secrecy in marriage. A Marriage of Conscience is one which is celebrated with the permission of the Ordinary of the place, in strict observance of the juridical form required by the common law, but in such a manner that it remains secret and unknown among the people. The necessary secrecy is to be obtained through the fact that the law calls for the omission of the banns of marriage and imposes upon the local Ordinary, the priest who assists at the marriage, the parties and the witnesses to the marriage, the grave obligation of keeping the fact of marriage concealed. The marriage is to be celebrated in secret, and the records pertaining to it are to be retained in special books in the Secret Archives of the diocese.[1]

There are different opinions as to why these Marriages are called "of Conscience." Some modern authors indicate that the chapter appearing in the Code, *De matrimonio conscientiae,*[2] is so styled for the twofold reason that these unions are by their nature secret, and

[1] Cf. Ayrinhac-Lydon, *Marriage Legislation,* p. 282; Payen, *De Matrimonio in Missionibus ac Potissimum in Sinis Tractatus Practicus et Casus* (3 vols., Zi-ka-wei: In typographia T'ou-sè-wè, 1929), II, n. 1934; Petrovits, *The New Church Law on Matrimony* (Philadelphia: John J. McVey, 1921), p. 368; Wernz-Vidal, *Ius Canonicum,* V, n. 565.

[2] Canons 1104; 1105; 1106; 1107.

that they bring with them the obligation of preserving secrecy on the part of all who witness them.[3] However, less recent authors, including the Cardinal who later as Pope Benedict XIV established the Marriage of Conscience juridically, determined the phrase "of Conscience" to indicate that the parties to such marriages were continually to keep in mind their obligations to each other and to their children.[4] Inasmuch as these opinions are not mutually exclusive, and since the acceptance of both does not involve any adherence to a contradiction, one could include the idea of the personal obligations of the parties to the marriage, as well as the all important note of secrecy which is binding on all who know of the union, in forming one's concept of what is meant by a Marriage "of Conscience."

No mistake should be made in considering the obligation in conscience incumbent on the parties. This manner of speaking is not meant to indicate that these persons are responsible only in their own consciences, or that they are obliged before God alone. Marriages of Conscience are entered in observance of the prescribed and commanded ecclesiastical substantial form, no exception from this form having been granted in their favor,[5] but they must also follow the unique regulations in their regard as found in the common law.[6] Therefore they bind before the Church as all other marriages which are entered in accord with her common law.[7]

The inauguration of this type of marriage was provoked by the lack of canonical provision for cases wherein secrecy was necessary. It was impossible in observing the form required by the Council of Trent to enter strictly secret marriages in the external form.[8] On the other hand, it had become increasingly apparent that there was a need for legislation which would comprehend and supply in cases wherein marriage and secrecy were both necessary, these two

[3] Payen, *De Matrimonio,* II, n. 1934; Petrovits, *The New Church Law on Matrimony,* p. 29.

[4] Benedictus XIV, *De Synodo Dioecesana,* lib. XIII, c. 23, n. 13; Andreucci, *Hierarchia Ecclesiastica,* lib. V, c. 5, n. 1; Mazzaeus, *De Matrimonio Conscientiae,* p. 9.

[5] Canon 1094.

[6] Canons 1104; 1105; 1106; 1107.

[7] Payen, *De Matrimonio,* II, n. 1934.

[8] Sess. XXIV, *de ref. matrim.* c. 1; *supra,* pp. 40-46.

elements not being reconcilable in public marriage.[9] The requirement of the observance of the substantial form of marriage was retained in the Papal document which originally established the Marriage of Conscience and proposed the procedure to be followed in the celebration of it.[10]

The encyclical letter *Satis Vobis* of Benedict XIV[11] is the forerunner of the present Code legislation regarding Marriages of Conscience. This document is the one which is proposed in the annotated Gasparri edition of the Code as the source from which the present law is principally drawn.[12] Substantially, then, the legislation of the Code has been borrowed from the encyclical legislation of Benedict XIV. From the time of the promulgation of the *Satis Vobis.*[13] till the present Code of Canon Law came into force[14] no new regulations were made, and no changes effected, regarding the administration of cases involving the use of the Marriage of Conscience. This expedient, however, found application in new conditions and previously unthought of circumstances which required the continued possibility of celebrating valid secret marriages long after the time of Benedict XIV.[15] It will be necessary therefore to depend on the old law, at

[9] Cappello, *Tractatus Canonico-Moralis De Sacramentis,* Vol. III, *De Matrimonio* (ed. quarta emendata et aucta, Romae: apud Aedes Univ. Gregorianae, 1939), III, pars II, n. 723; Wernz-Vidal, *Ius Canonicum,* V, n. 566.

[10] Benedictus XIV, ep. encycl. *Satis Vobis,* 17 nov. 1741—*Fontes,* n. 319.

[11] 17 nov. 1741—*Fontes,* n. 319.

[12] Cappello, *De Sacramentis,* III, pars II, n. 723; Vlaming, *Praelectiones Iuris Matrimonii Ad Normam Codicis Iuris Canonici* (3. ed., Bussum in Hollandia: Sumptibus Societatis Editricis Anonymae olim Paulus Brand, 1921), II, n. 593; Payen, *De Matrimonio,* II, n. 1935-1943; Wernz-Vidal, *Ius Canonicum,* V, n. 565; Ayrinhac-Lydon, *Marriage Legislation,* p. 282; Petrovits, *The New Church Law on Matrimony,* p. 368; Woywod, *A Practical Commentary on the Code of Canon Law* (New York: J. F. Wagner, 1925), I, 696.

[13] 17 nov. 1741—*Fontes,* n. 319.

[14] May 19, 1918.

[15] S. C. de Prop. Fide, instr. a. 1785—*Coll. S. C. P. F.* I, n. 571; Leo, litt. *Il divisamento,* 8 febr. 1893—*ASS,* XXV, (1894) 459; *Fontes,* n. 617.

least in some part, in indicating the correct interpretations of the present legislation, since, on the point in question, much has been incorporated into the new law that was originally in force quite some time before the Code.[16]

Article II. Changes from the Old Law

While the general character and requirements of the previous legislation regarding Marriages of Conscience have been retained in the law now in force, points which before were disputed have been settled. Certain additions have been made to the law. Perhaps most important, the regulations have been revised and evolved into a more concise and specific expression of the law.

The *Satis Vobis* placed the requirement for a *causa gravis, urgens et urgentissima*[17] which was not to be construed as simply any grave cause, but one which had allied with it other advantages, such as the legitimation of children, the relief from the seriously sinful state the spouses were living in, or the public good. In the Code it is found that the requisite cause must be *gravissima et urgentissima.*[18] This expression is peculiar to this one place in the common law.

Formerly those possessing the power to permit Marriages of Conscience included the Pope, all Patriarchs, Primates, Archbishops, and Bishops.[19] There was also the possibility of an appeal to the Metropolitan for permission in the instance of a refusal from the local Ordinary.[20] This possibility no longer exists. The local Ordinary alone may grant leave to enter a Marriage of Conscience in the external forum.[21] It was also quite generally agreed that the Vicar General could allow these marriages.[22] This problem is definitely settled in the Code by exluding him, except in cases in which he possesses a special mandate.[23]

[16] Canon 6, § 2, § 3.

[17] Benedictus XIV, ep. encycl. 17 nov. 1741, § 6—*Fontes,* n. 319.

[18] Canon 1104.

[19] Benedictus XIV, ep. encycl. *Satis Vobis,* 17 nov. 1741, § 7—*Fontes,* n. 319.

[20] Mazzaeus, *De Matrimonio Conscientiae,* p. 60.

[21] Canon 1104.

[22] Mazzaeus, *De Matrimonio Conscientiae,* p. 21.

[23] Canon 1104.

No demand for an express or explicit promise or oath of secrecy can be discovered in the *Satis Vobis*.[24] However, a post-Code permission to contract a Marriage of Conscience implies the necessity of exacting a promise of secrecy from all involved together with the grave obligation of preserving it.[25]

One case alone is mentioned in the old law in which the superior who allowed the Marriage of Conscience could divulge it on his own authority.[26] In the present legislation the power of the superior has been expanded in view of the law's indication of five instances in which, with the postulated facts verified, he may reveal the secret marriage.[27]

A single case is suggested in the *Satis Vobis* as having any claim and as being sufficiently grave to move a competent superior to grant permission for a Marriage of Conscience, that is, when a couple living together were reputed as married, though in fact, they were not, and desired to have their status rectified.[28] No enumeration of any kind of proposed cases appears in the legislation of the Code on the point in question. The case cited from the *Satis Vobis* has established a valuable precedent, as well as that document's injunction to use this form of marriage when the aforementioned status or other more urgent circumstances obtained. Under the present law any case which meets the requirements of the law may be submitted by way of petition to the local Ordinary, with the reasonable hope that the permission for a Marriage of Conscience will be granted.

The purpose of this Article is simply to indicate some major points of difference existing between the old law and the new law. Naturally the present legislation regarding Marriages of Conscience, though in some instances very similar to the previous law, cannot be discussed and interpreted without keeping in mind the necessary background of present day pertinent legislation, since it would not be at all unusual to discover divergent interpretation for laws which

24 *Supra*, p. 44.

25 Canon 1105.

26 Benedictus XIV, ep. encycl. *Satis Vobis*, 17 nov. 1741, § 13—*Fontes*, n. 319.

27 Canon 1106.

28 Benedictus XIV, ep. encycl. 17 nov. 1741, § 6—*Fontes*, n. 319.

are somewhat the same, but which were promulgated many years apart.

ARTICLE III. RELATION TO OTHER TYPES OF SECRET MARRIAGE

Before entering upon a detailed treatment of the Marriage of Conscience, one may usefully seek to establish exactly what is meant by this type of marriage in relation to other forms of marriage which have at times been confused with it. Not all marriages unknown to the public, or perfected with some care taken to maintain secrecy, fall into the category of Marriages of Conscience. The necessity of determining which Marriages are of Conscience and which are not is obvious, for only those unions which are entered in accord with the specific regulations pertaining to Marriages of Conscience are subject to the special law on this subject. They alone enjoy the privileges and are affected by the obligations adhering to this peculiar form of secret marriage. All others here mentioned are to be adjudged according to the principles of the common law regarding the sacrament of marriage. By the same token, it must be kept in mind that Marriages of Conscience also are subject to the common law of the church as are all other marriages, except in regard to the matters included under the clearly designated legislation contained in canons 1104, 1105, 1106, 1107.

Clandestine marriage in the accepted sense of that term is one which is contracted without the observance of the juridical form prescribed by the Church.[29] From this definition it appears that attempted marriages fall into the category of clandestinity if they are lacking in the requirements of the substantial form in their celebration, and in this sense alone are secret. Since many marriages are invalid because of lack of form, yet are known publicly, it would be of advantage to designate as clandestine only those marriages lacking in form which are attempted secretly, so that their celebration is not generally known. On the other hand, marriages known publicly to be lacking in form and therefore invalid could be designated

[29] Payen, *De Matrimonio,* I, n. 131; Wernz-Vidal, *Ius Canonicum,* V, n. 565; Petrovits, *The New Church Law On Matrimony,* p. 28.

as civil, common law, or simply attempted marriages, depending upon the circumstances.[30]

This terminology would be an aid in judging the guilt of the parties concerned. It would moreover be more in keeping with the historical concept of clandestinity, which has always indicated that the fact of marriage in a given case was not known.[31] Here especially the distinction would be helpful, since the Marriage of Conscience differs from its invalid counterpart, clandestine marriage, precisely on the points of substantial form and secrecy.[32] In the Marriage of Conscience the canonical form must be observed, and the manner of keeping the marriage secret is in no way decided by the parties, but the enactments of the law which indicate the method to be employed in entering and preserving these marriages in secrecy must be closely followed.[33]

Occult marriage is described in various ways by authors. The question which here finds application in their regard is whether or not all occult marriages are likewise Marriages of Conscience. Some authors make the general division between public and occult marriages, the occult ones being described as those which are celebrated without the previous proclamations and in accord with the prescriptions given for Marriages of Conscience.[34] This division is too inclusive in its description of the scope of the term "occult marriage." Not all occult marriages are Marriages of Conscience, if occult is accepted to mean merely that something is not known publicly. A simple subdivision into occult marriages in the strict sense, and in

30 Here *public* and *occult* are to be understood in the sense expressed in canon 2197 § 1, § 4.

31 *Supra,* p. 2.

32 Alford, *Jus Matrimoniale Comparativum* (New York: P. J. Kenedy & Sons, 1938), p. 22; Cappello, *De Sacramentis,* III, pars II, n. 743; Gasparri, *De Matrimonio,* n. 1243; Noldin-Schmitt, *Summa Theologiae Moralis,* III, n. 513; Wernz-Vidal, *Ius Canonicum,* V, n. 565.

33 Canon 1104.

34 Vermeersch, *Theologia Moralis,* III, n. 687; Wernz-Vidal, *Ius Canonicum,* V, n. 22.

the wide sense, as proposed by Cappello,[35] clarifies the situation and eliminates all confusion on this subject. Occult marriages in the wide sense are entered secretly, with a dispensation from the banns having been secured, before the proper pastor and witnesses. Nevertheless no promise or obligation of preserving secrecy is exacted, nor will an unusually serious reason be needed to proceed in this manner. Records of these marriages are to be entered in the parochial marriage register. An occult marriage in the strict sense is a Marriage of Conscience, accompanied with the pact of secrecy contracted in view of a most grave and urgent cause, attended with special permission and a unique form of registration, and fulfilling whatever other necessary canonical requirements may be demanded.

Morganatic marriage in its origin was a type of the Marriage of Conscience,[36] but this is no longer so.[37] In modern legislation the note of secrecy no longer adheres to a morganatic marriage in itself, though of course, if the conditions were fulfilled, the same union could be both morganatic and a Marriage of Conscience. Cappello [38] states that the morganatic marriage is entered with the observance of all the laws and solemnities of the Church. The restrictions involved are principally concerned with the civil effects. The Marriage of Conscience at present requires a dispensation from both the ordinary laws and usual solemnities, but once it is proved it obtains its full civil effects before the law.

There is a necessary relation existing between other types of marriage, such as mixed marriages, or marriages attempted in the face of a concealed diriment impediment, on the one hand, and the Marriage of Conscience on the other, in the same manner as there is a relation between these types of marriages along with the special circumstances which affect their validity or lawfulness, and marriage

[35] *De Sacramentis,* III, pars I, n. 49; also suggested in Alford, *Jus Matrimoniale Comparatum,* p. 22; Payen, *De Matrimonio,* I, n. 131, II, n. 1935.

[36] Schmalzgrueber, lib. IV, tit. I, n. 237.

[37] Cappello, *De Sacramentis,* III, pars II, n. 723; Noldin-Schmitt, *Summa Theologiae Moralis,* III, n. 513; Vermeersch, *Theologia Moralis,* III, n. 687.

[38] *Loc. cit.*

in general. The reason for precisely distinguishing clandestine, occult, and morganatic marriages from the type of union that forms the subject of this work is founded in the fact that these more than others displayed characteristics in their historical background which made them appear somewhat similar to Marriages of Conscience, and for this reason they have at times been confused with it.

CHAPTER VI

COMPETENT SUPERIOR, CAUSE, AND INVESTIGATION REQUIRED

Canon 1104.—Nonnisi ex gravissima et urgentissima causa et ab ipso loci Ordinario, excluso Vicario Generali sine speciali mandato, permitti potest ut *matrimonium conscientiae* ineatur, idest matrimonium celebretur omissis denuntiationibus et secreto, ad normam canonum qui sequuntur.

ARTICLE I. THE LOCAL ORDINARY ALONE IS COMPETENT TO PERMIT A MARRIAGE OF CONSCIENCE

THE language of canon 1104 specifically indicates which persons are competent to permit a Marriage of Conscience. The Ordinary of the place himself possesses this power, to the positive exclusion of the Vicar General. This placing of a restriction on the powers of the Vicar General which makes it impossible for him to act in certain cases without a special mandate is not uncommon in the Code.[1] However, in this place the exclusive power of the Ordinary of the place is accentuated by use of the word *ipso*. There is little doubt

[1] "Quae, mandatum speciale requirunt nunc in Codice *taxative* indicantur, nec ad alios casus sunt arbitrarie ex analogia extendenda", this list embraces canons 113, 115 with canon 455 and 1432, § 2; 187, § 1; 357, § 1; 455, § 3; 477, § 1; 686, § 4 with canon 492, § 1; 893, § 1; 958, § 1, n. 2; 1104; 1155, § 1; 1162, § 1; 1283, § 2; 1285, § 1; 1303, § 3; 1414, § 3; 1423, § 1; 1466, § 2; 1487, § 1; 2002; 2220, § 2; 2236, § 3; 2314, § 2,—Coronata, *Compendium Iuris Canonici* (Taurini: Marietti, 1937), I, n. 743; In addition to these, several other places have been cited which must be included even in an exhaustive listing of the places where a special mandate is required for the Vicar General to act, namely, canons 152, 343, 1; 370, 2; 959; 1191, 1; 1432, 2; 1573. Cf. Campagna, *Il Vicario Generale del Vescovo,* The Catholic University of America Canon Law Studies, n. 66 (Washington, D. C.: The Catholic University of America, 1931), pp. 130-131.

that this singular expression was incorporated into the law to impress upon those superiors who are given the competence to permit Marriages of Conscience that this grant has been made to them in a special manner, and its charge is not to be taken lightly.

The exclusive power of the local Ordinary, heightened by elimination of the Vicar General's capabilities in these matters, is so restricted by the law as given in canon 1104 as to remove adequately the possibility of the local Ordinary's delegating the power to grant these permissions for Marriages of Conscience to anyone. Dispensations are required in these cases from both the ordinary laws and the usual solemnities.[2] No one other than the Pope may dispense from the general laws of the Church even in a single case, unless the power necessary in a given instance or set of circumstances has been explicitly or implicitly granted, or is otherwise supplied.[3] The person explicitly designated to permit Marriages of Conscience is the local Ordinary,[4] who in this way obtains from the common law the faculty to grant the required dispensations from the universal law of the Church without resorting to a higher authority. Acting in this capacity the local Ordinary is exercising his ordinary power.[5]

Under the law those possessing the ordinary power of jurisdiction may delegate it to another in whole or in part, unless such delegation is expressly forbidden by law.[6] A prohibition of this nature is discovered in the limitation placed on Ordinaries who may permit Marriages of Conscience. The opinion of Blat[7] that the common faculties of Bishops to dispense from general laws are ordinary powers, but not capable of being delegated since they fall under the clause

[2] Cappello, De Sacramentis, III, pars II, n. 723.

[3] Canon 81.

[4] Canon 1104.

[5] Canon 197, § 1; Coronata, *Compendium Iuris Canonici,* I, n. 532; Vermeersch-Creusen, *Epitome,* I, n. 314.

[6] Canon 199, 1.

[7] *Commentarium Textus Codicis Iuris Canonici* (5 vols. in 6, Romae: Collegio Angelico, 1921-1927), II, n. 148.

"nisi aliud expresse iure caveatur," appears to be untenable.[8] In canon 1104, though, one not only does not find the phrase *"per se vel per alium,"* which phrase Blat requires for the possibility of delegation, but one also does not find a simple denial of the explicit power to delegate, the absence of which denial, so Kearney contends,[9] would most probably allow for the possibility of delegation. But canon 1104 states specifically that in no way *except* with permission of the Ordinary *himself,* or his Vicar General with a special mandate, may these Marriages of Conscience be allowed. Moreover, if the phrase *"ipsemet Ordinarius . . . invitet,"* in canon 2148, § 1, can be interpreted as precluding the possibility of delegation,[10] then the stronger phrase *"nonnisi . . . ab ipso loci Ordinario . . . permitti potest"* of canon 1104 most certainly precludes the possibility of delegation, but not the possibility of allowing the Vicar General to act from ordinary power with a special mandate, of which something will be said in another place.

If the Vicar General or another were habitually conceded the required delegation or mandate, the knowledge of the secret marriages would have to be extended to at least one other person than those mentioned in the law,[11] and the registration of the marriage would become more complicated since the Bishop or Apostolic Administrator would have to register the Marriage of Conscience contracted with the permission of the delegated authority or of the Vicar General,[12] or extend them the further privileges of entering the marriage and the subsequent baptismal records in the secret archives,[13] the power however, to inspect these records still remaining with the Bishop or Apostolic Administrator.

[8] A concise but definite rebuttal of this opinion is proposed in Kearney, *The Principles of Delegation* The Catholic University of America Canon Law Studies, n. 55 (Washington, D. C.: The Catholic University of America, 1929), pp. 79-82.

[9] *Loc. cit.*

[10] Connor, *The Administrative Removal of Pastors* The Catholic University of America Canon Law Studies, n. 104, (Washington, D. C.: The Catholic University of America, 1937), p. 83.

[11] Canon 1105.

[12] Canon 379, § 4.

[13] Louis, *Diocesan Archives,* p. 82-83.

The stress placed in the law on the exclusive power of the Ordinary of the place in permitting Marriages of Conscience can be explained again as a warning to others who might presume to arrogate to themselves faculties which they do not possess, even though formerly they might have, at least doubtfully, possessed them. Thus it is not left to the judgment of the pastor or parish priest to decide as to the advisability or need of a petitioning couple to contract a Marriage of Conscience.[14] The decision to grant permission in these cases is left to the prudence and wise judgment of the Ordinary of the place,[15] as is likewise the decision to divulge the fact of such a marriage when the circumstances warrant it.[16]

A. Who Are Competent Local Ordinaries

Since the competent superior named is the Ordinary of the place to the definite and specific exclusion of the Vicar General, some distinctions must be made to determine exactly the persons included under the term "Ordinary." The residential Bishop is commonly understood to be the local Ordinary, governing that portion of Christ's flock which is assigned to him by the *missio canonica*.[17]

According to canon 198, the term "local Ordinary" includes besides the residential Bishop, Abbots and Prelate *nullius*, and the Vicars General of these, Apostolic Administrators, Vicars and Prefects Apostolic within their respective territories, as well as those persons who, in case of the vacancy of the offices previously held bv the persons enumerated, succeed to the respective office by the provisions of the law or according to approved constitutions. These enjoy the same authority unless one or the other is expressly excluded, as the Vicar General is in the subject under discussion.

[14] Cappello, *De Sacramentis*, III, pars II, n. 724.

[15] Ayrinhac-Lydon, *Marriage Legislation*, p. 283.

[16] Canon 1106.

[17] Canon 335, § 1; Ottaviani, *Institutiones Iuris Publici Ecclesiastici* (2. ed., Civitas Vaticana; Typis Polyglottis Vaticana, 1935-1936), I, n. 220; Farrell, *The Rights and Duties of the Local Ordinary Regarding Congregations of Women Religious of Pontifical Approval*, The Catholic University of America Canon Law Studies, n. 128 (Washington, D. C.: The Catholic University of America Press, 1941), p. 1.

In listing the Ordinaries of places no mention was made in the canon of the Superior of Missions *sui iuris,* who are appointed directly by the Holy See and rule in the name of the Church itself.[18] From the text of the Instruction given in their regard it is quite obvious that, in reference to their powers, they were to be considered in the same category with Vicars and Prefects Apostolic,[19] and therefore as local Ordinaries.[20] In confirmation of this stand taken by the Sacred Congregation, this same Congregation issued a private response explaining the reason for which Superiors of Missions *sui iuris* were not included in the enumeration of Ordinaries as listed in canon 198, but it affirmed their status as that of Ordinaries.[21]

No mistake should be made in ruling these persons out as local Ordinaries because of the restriction of canon 198, § 2, which eliminates religious superiors from the ranks of local Ordinaries, and indicates that they are to be considered simply as Ordinaries. It is explicitly stated in the Instruction that the offices of Superior of the Mission and Superior of a Missionary Institute are distinct, and not in opposition. The jurisdiction of the Superior of the Mission extends to all priests and clerics in the designated territory regardless of the religious or diocesan attachments they may otherwise have.[22] All those above mentioned as local Ordinaries then, including Superiors of Missions *sui iuris,* are empowered to permit Marriages of Conscience in the territories under their jurisdiction, as are their successors.[23]

[18] Canon 1350; O'Brien, *The Exemption of Religious in Church Law* (Milwaukee: The Bruce Publishing Co., 1942), p. 222.

[19] S. C. de Prop. instr., 8 dec. 1929—*AAS,* XXII (1930), 111; also in Bouscaren, *Canon Law Digest* (2 vols., Milwaukee: The Bruce Publishing Co., 1934-1943), I, 637.

[20] Canon 198, § 1.

[21] S. C. de Prop. Fide, 31 aug. 1934—Bouscaren, *Canon Law Digest,* II, 121-122.

[22] O'Brien, *The Exemption of Religious in Church Law,* p. 223.

[23] Those who from the prescriptions of law or approved custom succeed to those mentioned above as local Ordinaries are :(a.) the chapter (of the cathedral, or of the Abbey or Prelacy *nullius*), until the election of the Capitular Vicar; (b.) the Capitular Vicar (in territories where a chapter is not established, the Diocesan Consultors and, in turn,

The term "Vicar General" includes in its concept not only Vicars General of residential Bishops, but also those of Abbots and Prelates *nullius*.[24] In the enumeration given in the canon, however, no provision was found for Vicars General who might be appointed by Vicars and Prefects Apostolic. This lack was supplied in the granting of permission to all Superiors of Missions to name Vicar and Prefect Delegates respectively, with all the faculties of Vicars General.[25] Finally, some years later, this same faculty was extended to Superiors of Missions *sui iuris,* who were allowed to name Superior Delegates in place of Vicars General.[26] Legislation given for Vicars General, then, comprehends and is applicable to Vicar, Prefect, and Superior Delegates.

The purpose of establishing definite classifications is easily discernible in the light of the precise and exacting language of canon 1104. All those who can be included under the general term "local Ordinary," with the exclusion of the Vicar General, may allow Marriages of Conscience in the territory over which they rule. At the same time it is necessary to keep in mind that in the term "Vicar General" are included all those named in place of Vicars General in mission territories. None of these is competent to allow Marriages of Conscience, lacking a special mandate. The exclusive character of the authority to permit these marriages in no way restrains the local Ordinary from delegating a priest to witness the Marriage of Conscience. If the local Ordinary so desired he could simply allow the celebrant to use his ordinary faculties, by which he is competent to witness all marriages in a certain place. In fact, the granting of permission in the law on the part of the local Ordinary presupposes

the elected Administrator take the places of the chapter and the Capitular Vicar respectively); (c.) the pro-Vicar; (d.) the pro-Prefect; (e.) the pro-Superior. Cf. canons 198, § 1, § 2; 309; 312; 327; 431; 432; S. C. de Prop. Fide, 8 dec. 1919—*AAS,* XII (1920), 120; Reilly, *The General Norms of Dispensation,* The Catholic University of America Canon Law Studies, n. 119 (Washington, D. C.: The Catholic University of America Press, 1939), p. 55.

24 Canon 198, § 1.

25 S. C. de Prop. Fide, 8 dec. 1919—*AAS,* XII (1920), 120.

26 S. C. de Prop. Fide, 7 nov. 1929—Bouscaren, II, 75-76.

and indicates the use of a priest other than the local Ordinary to witness the marriage.[27]

In each case the local Ordinary to be approached with the request for permission to enter a Marriage of Conscience is the proper Ordinary of the parties.[28] If the parties reside under different jurisdictions the proper Ordinary of the place where the marriage is to be entered should grant the permission, or either Ordinary if the ceremony is to take place outside both jurisdictions. A dispensation from the banns is included in the permission required, and for that reason it seems logical to follow the law which determines the proper Ordinaries in cases wherein the banns are not to be announced.[29] In any event, when dispensations are necessary, it would be more in keeping with the spirit of the law which is directed at maintaining secrecy, to secure them through the same Ordinary from whom the permission to enter the marriage is sought.[30]

B. Denial of Permission by the Local Ordinary

No restriction is placed on the will of the local Ordinary so that, given a sufficient cause, he must necessarily grant permission for a Marriage of Conscience. If, because of the peculiar conditions or circumstances of a case, he judges that a secret marriage would

[27] Canon 1105.

[28] Cf. canons 92, 93, 94, 95, regarding the method of determining who are proper Ordinaries; also Reilly, *The General Norms of Dispensation,* pp. 97-98.

[29] Canon 1028, § 2.

[30] If one of the proposed parties to the secret marriage is not a Catholic, the proper Ordinary of the Catholic party should be petitioned, who will be able to grant or secure the required dispensations and permit the marriage. Dispensations from an absolute impediment attaching to one party should be sought by that person's proper Ordinary; relative impediments may be dispensed through application to the proper Ordinary of either party. Ordinaries may, moreover, for just and grave reasons, dispense their own subjects even outside their territory, and other persons within it, in accord with the faculties granted them by the Holy Office as listed in the Quinquennial Faculties of Ordinaries.—Bouscaren, *Canon Law Digest,* II, 30-33; Cappello, *De Sacramentis,* III, pars I, n. 252; Wernz-Vidal, *Ius Canonicum,* V, n. 423.

not be opportune and suitable, he may decline to give the permission. This would quite often be the case in places in which it would be practically impossible to keep the fact of marriage a secret.[31] Upon receiving a denial of their petition the parties no longer may appeal to the Metropolitan for permission, as was formerly the practice.[32] Such an appeal would be in vain. The faculty of permitting Marriages of Conscience in suffragan sees is not included in the powers which Archbishops exercise in any diocese of their province other than their own.[33] Naturally this does not affect their granting of permissions in their own Archdioceses as local Ordinaries.[34] None the less, the fact of the local Ordinary's refusal to allow a Marriage of Conscience does not remove every possibility for the contraction of such a marriage.

Canons 43 and 44 include consideration of several sets of circumstances relative to the point of determining the effect which the refusal of a favor or dispensation by one superior will have on the subsequent concession made by another superior in the same matter. Some of the principles stated in these canons find application here. Several possibilities present themselves.

In the first place, if a local Ordinary refuses permission for a Marriage of Conscience, the permission may be sought in the external forum from the Sacred Congregation for the Discipline of the Sacraments,[35] and no mention need be made of a previous refusal.[36] The request for permission may also be presented in the internal forum, sacramental or extra-sacramental, to the Sacred Penitentiary. The procedure which Benedict XIV made possible was never revoked,[37] and therefore suffers no restriction in the present law.

31 Payen, *De Matrimonio,* II, n. 1944, 1945.

32 Cf. Mazzaeus, *De Matrimonio Conscientiae,* p. 60.

33 Canon 274; Coronata, *Compendium Iuris Canonici,* I, n. 650.

34 Canon 273.

35 Canon 249, 1.

36 Canon 43 does not require that the refusal of one's local Ordinary to a petition be mentioned when that same petition is later submitted to a competent Roman Congregation or Office.

37 Pius XI, const. *De Paenitentiaria Apostolica,* 25 martii 1935—*AAS,* XXVII (1935), 79; *Apollinaris,* VIII (1935), 181.

Secondly, if the parties have a domicile in one diocese, and, in addition, one or more quasi-domiciles in other jurisdictions, they may seek the favor in all the dioceses where they have not been refused, provided that they are subject to the proper Ordinaries of those dioceses by reason of quasi-domicile,[38] but in this case previous refusal must be mentioned, and the prospective grantor is not to concede permission till he has knowledge of the reasons for the previous denial from the Ordinary first petitioned.[39] Failure to observe these prescriptions, on the part of either petitioner or grantor, would make the concession unlawful, but of itself would not affect the validity of the mariage, or of the dispensations granted.[40]

Thirdly, if the parties are Catholics under different jurisdictions, then if the local Ordinary of one party has declined to permit the marriage, the local Ordinary of the other party, on the request of his subject, can grant the permission. No mention need be made in this instance of a previous refusal, for, although the original denial was made by a proper Ordinary to his subject, the second request is proposed not by this same subject, but by the subject of another proper Ordinary. The second petition thus remains an original petition. This case is not expressly comprehended by canon 44. The granting of the petition by the same Ordinary would, of course, involve having the marriage celebrated either where the permission was actually given, or outside the dioceses of both parties.[41]

Fourthly, if a Vicar General possesses the required mandate and refuses permission, the Bishop Ordinary would invalidly concede the permission if he has not been informed of the previous refusal. If the Bishop Ordinary makes the denial, the Vicar General can in no case grant it without the consent of the Bishop Ordinary, in spite of the fact that he might have a mandate.[42] If the Bishop Ordinary grants the favor knowing and expressing his desire to grant it re-

38 Canon 94.

39 Canon 44, 1.

40 Canon 11; Reilly, *The General Norms of Dispensation,* p. 86.

41 Canon 1028.

42 Canon 44, § 2.

gardless of the Vicar General's previous refusal, the favor is validly granted.[43]

C. Competence of the Vicar General Having a Special Mandate

A discussion of the nature of the power employed by the Vicar General when acting with a special mandate finds a place in this work. Essentially something must be said on this subject inasmuch as the canon designating the persons competent to permit Marriages of Conscience places this much controverted restriction of power explicitly in relation to the Vicar General.[44] The fundamental difference of opinion on this question is based on the varying interpretations given to canon 368, § 1. The reservation enunciated in that canon is exemplified in approximately thirty places throughout the Code of Canon Law, and as an exhaustive enumeration may not be extended to include other cases by way of analogy.[45] For the present purpose the best method, or at least the one to be followed, is to advance from a brief consideration of the opposing opinions to their application to the canon under discussion, in order to discover which opinion may best be adopted by Vicars General actually in possession of a mandate to permit a Marriage of Conscience.

The solution of the controversy depends on the extent of the power conceded in canon 368, § 1, not strictly on the nature of the power of the Vicar General. If the restriction placed in the demand for a special mandate limits the power of the office of the Vicar General to less than universal, it must be maintained that the special mandate indicates a delegation, and hence an act performed with a special mandate thus conferred would be the result

43 Cappello, Felix, M., *Summa Iuris Canonici,* (Vols. I-II, 2 ed., 1932-1934; Vol. III, 1936, Romae: apud Aedes Universitatis Gregorianae, 1932-1936), I, n. 247; Reilly, *The General Norms of Dispensation,* p. 88.

44 "Nonnisi ex gravissima et urgentissima causa et ab ipso loci Ordinario, *excluso Vicario Generali sine speciali mandato,* permtti potest ut matrimonium conscientiae ineatur. . ."—Canon 1104.

45 Coronata, *Compendium Iuris Canonici,* I, n. 743; Vermeersch-Creusen do not admit that this enumeration is exhaustive but do not offer to show why it is not.—*Epitome,* I, n. 479.

of delegated power. However, if the restriction is considered not as a subtraction, but as a suspension of power fundamentally universal, then the giving of the special mandate would simply effect that the suspension is thereby revoked. The Vicar General would then be authorized to act by reason of power fundamentally pertinent to his office. Such power, of course, would be ordinary, not delegated power.[46]

The power ordinarily erercised by Vicars General in their office is a vicarious ordinary power, which of necessity has inherent in it the characteristics of ordinary power, inasmuch as the former is simply a species of the latter.[47] Some concede that he uses this same ordinary power in executing a special mandate, whenever the mandate has been obtained for the case which postulates the presence of such a mandate.[48] Others insist that delegated power is employed in these instances.[49]

The present legislation on this matter in no way proposes to introduce a change in the office of the Vicar General.[50] However, because of the pre-Code uncertainty regarding the cases for which the Vicar General's power was suspended in view of a specifically required special mandate, a definite enumeration was supplied,[51] the office remaining as it was previously. This interpretation of canon 368, § 1, is certainly verified in the case under consideration. Benedict XIV granted to all Bishops the power to permit Marriages of

46 Roelker, "The Vicar General and the Special Mandate,"—*The Jurist,* II (1942), 347. This article contains a concise, but thorough and enlightening examination and comparison of the arguments advanced both for and against the use of ordinary power by the Vicar General acting with a special mandate.

47 Roelker, "The Vicar General and the Special Mandate,"—*The Jurist,* II (1942), 348.

48 Coronata, *Compendium Iuris Canonici,* I, n. 743; Vermeersch-Creusen, *Epitome,* I, n. 479; Maroto, *Institutiones Iuris Canonici ad Normam Novi Codicis* (Matriti: 1919-1921), I, n. 699; Wernz-Vidal, *Ius Canonicum,* II, n. 639, 640.

49 Chelodi, *Ius De Personis* (Tridenti: Libr. Edit. Tridentum, 1922), p. 330; Kearney, *The Principles of Delegation,* pp. 72-74.

50 Wernz-Vidal, *Ius Canonicum,* II, n. 638.

51 Coronata, *Compendium Iuris Canonici,* I, n. 743; Vermeersch-Creusen, *Epitome,* I, n. 479.

Conscience in their own dioceses.[52] This power was generally believed to be possessed also by Vicars General, and Vicars Capitular *sede vacante*.[53] Again, persons desirous of entering a Marriage of Conscience, being refused by the Bishop, by the *Vicar General*, or by the Vicar Capitular *sede vacante*, could appeal to the Metropolitan.[54] However, though apparently this power was not denied to the Vicar General, it was hoped that Bishops would reserve its use to themselves.[55]

This restriction was actually placed in the Code in canon 1104, though the reservation thus implemented in the law did not in any way alter the fundamental extent of the office of the Vicar General. He still possesses universal jurisdiction, based on the correct interpretation of canon 368, § 1.[56] Therefore, no substantial change has been introduced by the Code. The extent of the office of Vicar General is as universal as previously, but the use of his powers in certain cases has been suspended. In the case of Marriages of Conscience, the reservation of this power of the Vicar General had always been desirable, as has already been demonstrated; in the present law it has simply been made definite. Acting with a special mandate, then, in permitting a Marriage of Conscience, the Vicar General would employ, now as before, ordinary power. Since canon 368, § 1, specifically determines a law which for some time had been essentially observed in an indeterminate number of cases, the nature of the law now in force is to be judged from the old law.[57]

The contention of Wernz-Vidal, that in canon 368, § 1, the power of Bishops to reserve certain acts to themselves by suspending the ordinary power of the Vicar General is similar to the restriction placed by the special mandate,[58] is here supported. Formerly

52 Ep. encycl. *Satis Vobis,* 17 nov. 1741—*Fontes,* n. 319.

53 Mazzaeus, *De Matrimonio Conscientiae,* p. 19.

54 Mazzaeus, *De Matrimonio Conscientiae,* p. 62.

55 "Optandum tamen esset, ut Episcopi potestatem hanc sibi reservarent."—Mazzaeus, *op. cit.,* p. 19.

56 Roelker, "The Vicar General and the Special Mandate",—*The Jurist,* II (1942), 353-355.

57 Canon 6, 2°.

58 *Ius Canonicum,* II, n. 640.

the Vicar General could permit Marriages of Conscience, but Bishops were cautioned to reserve this power. If they reserved it, they did not limit the extent of the Vicar General's office, any more than they would in the present legislation if they decided to reserve to themselves certain acts attached to the office of the Vicar General by the common law.[59] Upon deciding to remove such a reservation the Bishop simply "removes an obstacle which has prevented the office from possessing the amplitude of power conceded to it by law." [60]

The Vicar General permitted Marriages of Conscience in the past, but the Bishop could, and it was desired that he should reserve that power. Ordinary power was employed by the Vicar General in this regard, even when he would have had to seek a release from the Bishop's reservation if one existed. There is no reason to believe otherwise, for the need of a special mandate was not then prescribed by the law. There is likewise no reason for proposing that the Code effected a cancellation of this power. In the present there exists in the law the formal reservation which was formerly possible and desired. Such a restriction was probably existent in some places, since this permission was certainly always one which was to be given under the personal supervision of the Bishop because of the secret and unusual character of what was entailed when the granted permission was put in use.[61]

Since the nature of the law has not changed, but rather the pre-existing law has now become specific in the demand for a special mandate, resort must again be had to the old law for a correct interpretation.[62] In the old law the Vicar General allowed these marriages on his own authority, or after being released from the Bishop's reservation, but in both instances he exercised an ordinary power. There is a similar application in the present law. Now as

[59] Canon 368, § 1.

[60] This much is admitted by Kearney, though in his work he denies the parity between the right to reserve, and the restriction placed by common law demanding a special mandate.—*The Principles of Delegation*, pp. 73-74.

[61] Benedictus XIV, ep. encycl. *Satis Vobis*, 17 nov. 1741, § 6—*Fontes*, n. 319.

[62] Canon 6, § 2.

formerly the Vicar General, when he acts with a special mandate, acts with ordinary power. The same power which he employs in exercising rights he possesses from the common law is also the power which he exercises upon the recall of a reservation of the rights which the Bishop previously reserved to himself.

There is an opinion that the phrase *"nisi ex mandato speciali"* is employed to make it perfectly clear that delegation of the Vicar General is not prohibited, since it might be doubted whether a Bishop could delegate the Vicar General for such matters.[63] This appears somewhat difficult to understand. If the phrase is meant to confer the right and the power to effect a delegation in certain cases, then it cannot be asserted with reference to the general powers of delegation which Ordinaries have[64] that "nothing can be deduced from the presence or absence of explicit power to delegate."[65]

In the case under consideration in this work the local Ordinaries can permit Marriages of Conscience, *"excluso Vicario Generali sine speciali mandato."* This restricts the Vicar General's power to act as Vicar General, but in no way renders him incapable of receiving delegation, if delegation were possible. Certainly the Vicar General can not be denied the potentiality of using delegated power if it can be given, any more than it must be denied to any other priest. Canon 199, § 1, does not exclude him. He can be delegated to act as any other priest in the instances commonly allowable. However, this is not exactly the point of the discussion. When a special mandate is required a simple delegation will not suffice, or there would be no reason for placing the clause demanding a mandate. Something in addition is required on the part of the recipient of the commission to act. The peculiar power possessed by the Vicar General, not possesesd by other priests, is ordinary power.[66]

In the light of canon 1104 the Vicar General who has a special mandate can not act in virtue of delegated power, because the possibility of the Bishop's naming a delegate of any kind has been excluded in view of the norm of canon 199, 1, as applied to canon

[63] Kearney, *The Principles of Delegation,* p. 73.

[64] Canon 199, § 1.

[65] Kearney, *op. cit.* p. 81.

[66] Canon 366, § 1.

1104.[67] The local Ordinary himself, though his power of delegating has been effectively precluded in this case, may permit Marriages of Conscience. Therefore, given a special mandate the Vicar General may allow a Marriage of Conscience in the exercise of his office as a local Ordinary using ordinary power, since the possibility of his employing a delegated power in this instance has been eliminated. Neither he nor anyone may be delegated to permit a Marriage of Conscience. Therefore, in executing the special mandate conferred on him, the Vicar General exercises an ordinary vicarious power, which is native to the office of a Vicar General, and which is consequently identified with and a species of ordinary power.[68]

Article II. A Most Grave and Most Urgent Cause Required

In composing the legislation which was to signalize the requirements and limitations imposed on those local Ordinaries empowered to permit Marriages of Conscience, the formulators of the law seem to have followed the much practiced and most commendable habit of putting the most important things in the primary positions. The initial demand in the law is for a cause which is most grave and, at the same time, most urgent.[69] Not only is any specific phrase couched in these words found nowhere else in the Code, but no expression closely akin to it is in evidence in the present law.

This clause originated in a somewhat identical wording with Benedct XIV, who prescribed a cause *gravis, urgens, et urgentissima.*[70] Therefore, the reasons for incorporating this phrase in a very similar but perhaps more concise form were historical as well as canonical. Such a statement does not posit a contradiction in any sense, since the implications of the law as it stands are the same in any event. Here is another indication of what has been stated previously to the effect that the existing law was adopted in great part from the law of Benedict XIV on the subject, in fact, in many respects the two laws, old and new, are identical.

67 *Supra*, pp. 58-60.

68 Canon 197, 2.

69 "Nonnisi ex gravissima *et* urgentissima causa. . ."—Canon 1104.

70 Ep. encycl. *Satis Vobis,* 17 nov. 1741, § 7—*Fontes,* n. 319.

No authors have chosen to expand on precisely what the combination *causa gravissima et urgentissima* technically indicates, although some propose a few traditional cases. But by invoking the often safer norms of the common law in its relations to the case at hand one is enabled of himself, with little difficulty, to deduce at least in great part what manner of cause is needed by a competent local Ordinary before he can allow a Marriage of Conscience. If the words under consideration, then, are to be understood correctly, and their implications exposed usefully, primary attention must be given to the words themselves, as they appear in their own text and context. After that, deductions may be introduced from the use of identical or similar words in other laws, from the purpose of the law, the circumstances pertinent, and from the mind of the lawgiver.[71]

The cause [72] demanded in this case, as in all cases wherein a matter of dispensation is involved, must, as viewed frow the approach of the common law, be just and reasonable.[73] However, when the Code makes the provision that a just and reasonable cause must be present to justify the granting of a dispensation, it also establishes the norm in accordance with which the justice and reasonableness of the cause is to be weighed. Not only is the person who dispenses expected to consider whether a reasonable motive is presented for departing from the common norm, but he must also weigh in the balance the cause proposed and the gravity of the law from which the dispensation is sought, in order to determine whether a due proportion exists between the two.[74]

This obligation is incumbent upon the superior, on whose vigilance and understanding of the cause, in every case, will turn the

[71] Canon 18.

[72] For a treatment of the aspects of cause which must be comprehended in questions of dispensation, i.e., motivating and accessory, intrinsic and extrinsic, etc., cf. Reilly, *The General Norms of Dispensation,* pp. 106-107.

[73] Canon 84, § 1.

[74] ". . . habita ratione gravitatis legis a qua dispensatur; alias dispensatio ab inferiore data illicita et invalida est".—Canon 84, § 1.

valid use of the powers entrusted to him.[75] Not all causes, then, are of the same gravity, nor will causes which are specifically the same be regarded equally motivating in all cases.[76] There are some laws more proximately connected with the common good than others. Certainly one can make this statement concerning the marriage laws of the Church, with perhaps even more justification than in relation to other laws. Marriage is the divinely instituted foundation of the christian family without which, in short, there could be no common good. Church law has always recommended, and long specifically demanded, public marriage.[77]

When it became apparent that there were some circumstances in which marriage was most necessary in order to avoid spiritual and temporal hardships which would otherwise befall the prospective parties and the children, and yet a union could not be perfected unless strict secrecy was observed, as in all matters, so in the present concern, ecclesiastical authorities wisely made ample but careful provision. The greatest care was necessary, inasmuch as secrecy in marriage was contrary to the traditional attitude of the Church, and the normal manner of safeguarding the common good.

For these reasons it seems that the legislator employed a unique but graphic combination of words, drawn principally from pre-Code legislation, in qualifying the requirement of a cause for the valid celebration of a secret marriage. Before there be granted the petition of the parties who seek to enter a Marriage of Conscience, the cause presented must manifest two determinate qualities. It must be grave beyond the ordinary, that is, it must be most grave, and marriage must be of paramount and immediate necessity. A mar-

[75] In granting these permissions for Marriages of Conscience, in accord with the powers conferred on him by the common law, the local Ordinary acts in virtue of vicarious ordinary power, and as such is an inferior. Therefore he requires a proportionately just and reasonable cause to act. Cicognani, *Canon Law,* p. 855; Beste, *Introductio in Codicem,* (Collegeville, Minn.: St. John's Abbey, 1938), p. 129; Coronata, *Compendium Iuris Canonici,* I, n. 532.

[76] Cicognani, *Canon Law,* p. 852; Beste, *Introductio in Codicem,* p. 129; Cappello, *De Sacramentis,* III, pars I, n. 257; Wernz-Vidal, *Ius Canonicum,* V, n. 149.

[77] Conc. Trident., sess. XXIV, *de ref. matrim.,* c. 1.

riage which is to be entered in strict secrecy may not be allowed for a most grave cause *or* a most urgent one. Both qualities must concur before the desired permission can be validly given.[78]

When it has been the desire of the lawmaker to indicate necessity which will not brook any delay without serious consequences he has employed various forms of the same word which is indicative of urgency. Extraordinary faculties to dispense from the form and the impediments to marriage are conferred on local Ordinaries *urgente mortis periculo.*[79] Alienation of ecclesiastical property requires a *iusta causa, idest urgens necessitas,*[80] which is to be understood in the sense of a case which must be taken care of here and now, if its handling and solution is not to come too late.[81] In the event that serious spiritual harm will be caused in delay, the confessor may use the special faculties conceded to him *in casibus urgentioribus* to absolve from certain censures.[82] All of these passages stress the notion of the need of immediate action, though none embodies use of the imperative superlative *urgentissima.* Canon 1104 alone employs this word. The obvious meaning is the correct one. In Marriages of Conscience the cause alleged must combine with its most grave character the connotation that any delay would result in real harm.

From what has been said it is evident that the causes usually regarded as sufficient for the seeking of a dispensation from the impediments to marriage, or from the proclamation of the banns, would not be acceptable if submitted by themselves in a request for the contraction of a Marriage of Conscience.[83] However, there does not

78 Canon 1104.

79 Canon 1043.

80 Canon 1530, § 2.

81 Heston, *The Alienation of Church Property in the United States,* The Catholic University of America Canon Law Studies, n. 132 (Washington, D. C.: The Catholic University of America Press, 1941), p. 84.

82 Canon 2254.

83 Cf. Quigley, *A Summary of the Canon Law on Matrimonial Impediments and Dispensations* (2 ed. Philadelphia: The Dolphin Press, 1942), pp. 10-13, for a brief and easily understandable treatment of the causes for dispensation. Causes five and six, namely, "convalidatio matrimonii attentati coram ministello" and "convalidatio matrimonii attentati

exist any enumeration of causes upon which one could rely as being complete, or to which one could refer as touching all possible contingencies. Certain cases have been established, though, in which a Marriage of Conscience is not only allowable but even commendable. This list has expanded somewhat over the years since the inauguration by Benedict XIV of the secret marriage to which the juridical effects of the external forum were attached.[84]

A review of the actual circumstances in which these secret unions have been permitted will serve to demonstrate which causes have in the past been considered to entail the extraordinary degree of gravity and urgency required, as well as to suggest present day circumstances in which a petition to enter a strictly secret marriage may be heard and granted.

The mere desire on the part of the parties to keep their marriage secret and unknown among their friends, the intention being that of surprising them in a year or so, quite apparently, can not be construed as a sufficient reason for seeking permission to enter a Marriage of Conscience.[85] With equal truth it can be reiterated that by no means all of the causes ordinarily regarded as sufficient for the granting of dispensations will form adequate grounds. For example, a girl's limited prospects of marriage, her advance in years beyond an age suited for marriage, or the insufficiency of her dowry would of themselves not be grave and urgent enough to warrant permitting a Marriage of Conscience. No commonplace or ordinary cause, therefore, should ever influence the local Ordinary.[86]

The only case mentioned specifically by Benedict XIV as sufficiently grave and urgent to require permission for entering a strictly secret marriage was taken from the practice and procedure of the

coram magistratu", on page ten of this work, which concern the convalidation of attempted marriages, would in some instances form a cause grave enough for use in a petition which seeks to obtain permission for contraction of a Marriage of Conscience. However, the requirement of extreme urgency must also be present.

[84] Ep. encycl. *Satis Vobis*, 17 nov. 1741—*Fontes*, n. 319; Benedictus XIV, *De Synodo Dioecesana*, lib. XIII, tit. XXIII, n. 13.

[85] Ayrinhac-Lydon, *Marriage Legislation*, p. 283.

[86] Benedictus XIV, ep. encycl. *Satis Vobis*, 17 nov. 1741, § 6—*Fontes*, n. 319.

Sacred Penitentiary, which had established the precedent of granting permission in circumstances wherein a man and woman were publicly living as husband and wife, and whom everyone believed to be married, while in reality they were not.[87] This is the case most generally cited by authors even in the present day as the most suitable one.[88]

Several other sets of circumstances have been proposed by modern authors as fulfilling the conditions required in establishing a cause most grave and most urgent. A nobleman who is rightfully desirous of marrying an obscure woman, but at the same time strives to avoid the disapproval and disinheritance of his family, could be given permission to enter a Marriage of Conscience.[89] A situation such as the one just described may appear rather to demand a morganatic marriage. This is quite true, but though marriage in such a case could be styled morganatic, yet if it were entered in strict secrecy it would be primarily and canonically a Marriage of Conscience. Originally morganatic marriage always involved secrecy, but not in the present legislation.

87 "Id enim, ut ad praescriptum Sacrorum Canonum licite fieri possit, non satis est obvia quaevis, et vulgaris causa, sed gravis, urgens, et urgentissima requiritur. A Sacro Nostrae Poenitentiariae Tribunali, eo potissimum casu fit potestas ita celebrandi Matrimonium, quo vir, et femina in figura Matrimonii publici degentes, et de quibus nulla viget criminis suspicio, in occulto tamen Concubinatu perseverent. Facile enim quisque coniiciet, quam absonum esset, eos, a statu damnationis per gratiam Sacramenti revocandos, ad publice contrahendum Matrimonium praeviis Denunciationibus compelli. Hanc vero praxim Vobis duximus proponendam, non quia dispensatio praemisso casui solum congruat, cum alii similes, et fortasse urgentiores esse possint, in quibus dispensari expediat; . . ."—ep. encycl. *Satis Vobis,* 17 nov. 1741, § 6—*Fontes,* n. 319.

88 Cappello, *De Sacramentis,* III, pars II, n. 723; Rossi, *De Matrimonio Celebratione iuxta Codicem Iuris Canonici* (Romae: Fredericus Pustet, 1924), p. 126; Vermeersch-Creusen, *Epitome,* II, n. 410; Vlaming, *Praelectiones Iuris Matrimonii,* II, n. 593; Wernz-Vidal, *Ius Canonicum,* V, n. 567; Ayrinhac-Lydon, *Marriage Legislation,* p. 283; Petrovits, *The New Church Law on Matrimony,* p. 30; Woywod, *Practical Commentary on the Code,* I, 696.

89 Payen, *De Matrimonio,* II, n. 1942; Vlaming, *Praelectiones Iuris Matrimonii,* II, n. 593; Wernz-Vidal, *Ius Canonicum* V, n. 567.

There is no definite procedure or special legislation indicated in the Code for these marriages if they are entered publicly. But if they are entered in secrecy they become a species of the Marriage of Conscience, and thus must be entered in compliance with the regulations affecting strictly secret marriages. Morganatic Marriages are not of frequent occurrence in our times, and it would indeed be rare to discover that one had been celebrated in our country. However, related cases involving unjust and violent opposition to marriage, manifested because of disparate social and economic conditions by the parents of the parties desiring marriage is not unheard of.[90] If the persons involved have had children, or have been manifestly the proximate cause of mutual sin which will not be desisted from, a Marriage of Conscience would rectify the spiritual lives of the parties, and legitimize the children if that proved necessary. It would also insure the inheritance of the children. Sometimes a marriage of this type need only be kept secret a relatively short time, one or two years, till the opposition is removed. In the meanwhile the parties avoid the always proximate danger of spiritual ruin.

Another proposed cause, carrying with it the note of serious temporal loss, is the case of a widow who is desirous of marrying again, but in so doing would lose the care of her children, and the supervision of their temporal goods, or both.[91] Under most systems of government in the present day the hardship of separating a widow from her children because she has contracted a second marriage is not imposed by civil authorities. Regarding the temporal loss though, it would be quite possible for a husband to frame his last will and testament in such a way that on remarrying after his death his widow would be legally divested of a great share of property otherwise hers under his will. But even in this instance a wife would ordinarily still retain her right to a dower share of her deceased husband's estate, which claim could not be eliminated by a contrary

[90] Wernz-Vidal, *Ius Canonicum*, V, *loc. cit.;* Woywod, *Practical Commentary on the Code, loc. cit.*

[91] Cappello, *loc. cit.;* Chelodi, *Ius Matrimoniale* (ed. quarta, recognita et aucta a V. Dalpiaz, Tridenti: Libreria Moderna Editrici A. Ardesi, 1937), n. 143; Payen, *loc. cit.;* Wernz-Vidal, *loc. cit.;* Ayrinhac-Lydon, *loc. cit.*

testamentary disposition.[92] Thus the temporal loss would not constitute an extraordinary problem, nor would a new marriage leave her in abject poverty.

A condition somewhat allied to the one just detailed would exist when a widow wishes to enter marriage, but knows that she would be unable to conduct a business or retain the employment necessary for the support of herself and her children.[93] Nau says that the desire of a married woman to preserve her employment would only in very rare cases be a sufficient reason to keep the marriage secret.[94] Perhaps this is true in itself, but if in addition secret marriage would eliminate secret concubinage in such circumstances, the local Ordinary would be justified in prudently permitting the Marriage of Conscience.

If a member of the armed forces is desirous of marrying a woman who lacks the dowry prescribed for wives who are parties to military marriages, some say he could allege his condition as a valid reason for requesting permission to enter a Marriage of Conscience, particularly when marriage is necessary to remove the parties from the seriously sinful state in which they are living.[95] Such a condition could hardly arise in this country, since civil laws demanding dowries of those marrying men in the armed forces do not exist. In countries where they do exist it remains for the local Ordinary to decide whether the nature of each case warrants his permission for a Marriage of Conscience.

This type of marriage has been recommended as a remedy when marriage is most necessary for the personal salvation of the parties, and yet they are barred by civil law impediments from contracting marriage.[96] Circumstances of this nature are not at all unheard of in the United States. Of course the marriage legislation in each

92 Hannan, *The Canon Law of Wills,* The Catholic University of America Canon Law Studies, n. 86 (Washington, D. C.: The Catholic University of America, 1934), pp. 93, 105.

93 Ayrinhac-Lydon, *Marriage Legislation,* p. 283.

94 *Marriage Laws of the Code* (2. ed., Cincinnati: Frederick Pustet, 1934), p. 165.

95 Payen, *loc. cit.;* Vlaming, *loc. cit;* Wernz-Vidal, *loc. cit;* Petrovits, *The New Church Law on Matrimony,* p. 30.

96 Payen, *loc. cit;* Vlaming, *loc. cit;* Petrovits, *loc. cit.*

of the States and possessions of the United States comprises a set of statutes differing from those of its neighbors. Generally considered however there are between civil and ecclesiastical law many points of conflict which are especially embodied in the laws setting forth the matrimonial impediments.[97]

The civil law, while in most instances making allowance for the fact that some of its enactments are at times arduous and difficult to bear in certain individual cases, deplores this condition as an inevitable evil of all law, but in no case provides for the possibility of obtaining a dispensation.[98] An enigma thus presents itself, though not too difficult of solution by the local Ordinary when he is faced with such a problem. If the spiritual welfare of the parties demands that they be married, and marriage is possible under the laws of the Church but not under the laws of the state, there arises an unavoidable conflict between the duty of conscience and the law of the state.[99] Cognizant of the penalties, but intent upon the preservation of right order one could apply the words of St. Peter, "If it be just in the sight of God, to hear you rather than God, judge ye." [100] Use of a Marriage of Conscience in these cases therefore is justified. A more detailed treatment of this question, and the particular problem encountered in relation to it in the United States, will appear in a subsequent chapter.

Only one case was proposed specifically in the *Satis Vobis* [101] as containing the elements postulated for securing permission to contract a Marriage of Conscience. But this case was given as a demonstrative example. Not only was no restriction placed on the number and type of cases which might fall within the scope of the regulations regarding these marriages, but definite instruction was offered to the effect that the method detailed could be employed in cases other than the one indicated which cases might in some instances be even more

[97] Alford, *Ius Matrimoniale Comparatum* (New York: P. J. Kenedy & Sons, 1938), pp. 58-61, 141-177.

[98] Alford, *Ius Matrimoniale Comparatum,* p. 177.

[99] Woywod, *Practical Commentary on the Code,* I, 698.

[100] Acts, IV, 19.

[101] Benedictus XIV, ep. encycl, 17 nov. 1741, § 6—*Fontes,* n. 319.

urgent than the one illustrated.[102] The Code, recasting the previous legislation, omits the suggestion of any case whatsoever. There is likewise no enumeration of causes in evidence in the pertinent canons,[103] either comprehensive or only demonstrative.[104] Therefore, no limit was placed either in the old or the new law. Naturally certain cases recur almost in any age, and the rules are always applicable in such instances. But others may develop from conditions and circumstances peculiar to the times. It is the obligation of the local Ordinary to decide whether a case is included in the prescriptions enacted for Marriages of Conscience.

Benedict XIV based his indicated case on the practice of the Sacred Tribunal of the Penitentiary.[105] That Tribunal before the time of Benedict obviously had been competent in granting permissions to contract strictly secret marriages, and it still is in our days.[106] Following the style and practice of this Tribunal, therefore, in determining whether a given case falls within the local Ordinary's competence would be in accord with an essential principle of law.[107]

Frequently diocesan tribunals are presented with cases involving two persons who have been living in concubinage, one of whom was previously married. The former marriage standing in the way of convalidation, consequently also in the way of cessation of the concubinage through subsequent marriage, sometimes at first offers great probability of being declared null upon being investigated. However,

102 "Hanc vero praxim Vobis duximus proponendam, non quia dispensatio praemisso casui solum congruat, cum alii similes, et fortasse urgentiores esse possint, in quibus dispensari expediat";—Benedictus XIV, ep. encycl. *Satis Vobis,* 17 nov. 1741, § 6—*Fontes,* n. 319; Benedictus XIV, *De Synodo Dioecesana,* lib. XIII, tit. XXIII, n. 13; Mazzaeus, *De Matrimonio Conscientiae,* p. 57.

103 Canons 1104, 1105, 1106, 1107.

104 Cappello, *De Sacramentis,* III, pars II, n. 723; Payen, *De Matrimonio,* II, n. 1941.

105 Ep. encycl. *Satis Vobis,* 17 nov. 1741, § 6—*Fontes,* n. 319.

106 Kubelbeck, *The Sacred Penitentiaria and Its Relations to Faculties of Ordinaries and Priests,* The Catholic University of America Canon Law Studies, n. 5 (Washington, D. C.: The Catholic University of America, 1918), p. 39.

107 Canon 20; Cappello, *De Sacramentis,* III, pars II, n. 723.

because of the lack of required testimony, or of documents, or because all the required canonical procedure cannot be followed for reasons beyond the control of the petitioner, the case, after having gone through the preliminary stages, reaches the point beyond which no further testimony can be adduced or any progress made. The diocesan court realizes its incapability of passing judgment. The elements of proof have been alleged, but only partly and insufficiently presented. There are some indications of the truth of the facts proposed by the party seeking to be declared free of the first alleged earlier invalid marriage, and there is also no reason to doubt his good faith, since all that is desired is a valid marriage with a present consort, if this is possible, and the legitimation of the children born of the concubinal union.

In cases of this kind, the previous marriage which is being investigated will on repeated occasions not be known in the community. In fact, the situation is ordinarily one in which the party who seeks the favor of the Church is looked upon in the community as validly married to the person with whom he is living. The possibility of appealing to the Sacred Tribunal of the Penitentiary remains to the persons involved. This Tribunal is competent in all cases that are not of the external forum, but of the forum of conscience both sacramental and extra-sacramental. It acts in occult cases through the confessor, and in public cases through the Ordinary.[108] The Sacred Penitentiary likewise dispenses or grants faculties to dispense from the publication of the banns and from occult impediments which impede or invalidate marriage, [109] even in view of contracting a Marriage of Conscience.[110] Being apprised of the facts in cases such as the one outlined above, the Tribunal of the Sacred Penitentiary has not hesitated to act within its competence in granting the dispensations required, and in allowing a new marriage in the internal forum to relieve the consciences of the parties and to legitimize their children when this is possible. However, in these same circumstances the local Ordinary is not competent to allow Marriages of Conscience in the

108 Kubelbeck, *The Sacred Penitentiaria and Its Relation to the Faculties of Ordinaries and Priests,* p. 36.

109 Cappello, *De Sacramentis,* III, pars I, n. 227.

110 Kubelbeck, *op. cit.,* p. 39.

external forum, though if the Holy See deemed it wise, it would be of great advantage to local Ordinaries if they possessed the faculties to grant the required dispensations and permit Marriages of Conscience, if in their prudent discretion no previous bond existed in cases proposed to them as the one above detailed.

Article III. Necessity of Making a Pre-nuptial Investigation

All pastors and all local Ordinaries may validly and licitly assist at the marriages of their subjects within their respective jurisdictions.[111] However, if the marriage be a Marriage of Conscience, then pastors may not make use of their power to assist at the marriage without receiving the previous permission of the local Ordinary himself.[112] In every case the pastor who has the right to assist at a marriage must pursue a diligent pre-nuptial investigation.[113] The local Ordinary is included under the term pastor.[114] Acting as a pastor, then, in a case pertaining specifically to himself, he may not permit marriage till the results of the pre-nuptial investigation prove favorable in his eyes.[115] This obligation of perfecting a pre-nuptial inquisition in any case is a grave one,[116] and it is incumbent on the local Ordinary personally to assure himself on the results of the inquisition in cases of Marriage of Conscience.[117]

The local Ordinary should make the investigation personally, or

[111] Canons 1095, § 1; 1097, § 1.

[112] Canon 1104.

[113] Canon 102.

[114] Donovan, *The Pastor's Obligation in Pre-nuptial Investigation*, p. 66.

[115] Canon 1096, § 2.

[116] Benedictus XIV, encycl. epist. *Etsi minime,* 7 febr. 1742, § 11—*Fontes,* n. 324; Gasparri, *De Matrimonio,* I, n. 130; Cappello, *De Sacramentis,* III, pars II, n. 146; Payen, *De Matrimonio,* I, n. 376; Ayrinhac-Lydon, *Marriage Legislation,* p. 26; S. C. de *Sacr., instr., De normis a parocho servandis in peragendis canonicis investigationibus antequam nupturientes ad matrimonium ineundum admittat,* 29 iun. 1941, 2, 3—*AAS,* XXXIII (1941), 297-298; *The Jurist,* II (1942), Supplement, pp. 1-2.

[117] Cappello, *De Sacramentis,* III, pars II, n. 723; Wernz-Vidal, *Ius Canonicum,* V, n. 567.

at least review the results of the investigation made by the pastor who will assist at the marriage when permission is granted. The purpose of the investigation is, of course, to establish the freedom of the parties to be married, and the principles and recommendations governing all pre-nuptial investigations should be adhered to as much as possible.[118] In all instances wherein a dispensation is sought an investigation into the truth of the causes alleged for the dispensation constitutes part of the pre-nuptial investigation.[119] Because of the insistence on a most grave and a most urgent cause in questions of Marriages of Conscience, special attention must be given by the local Ordinary to scrutinizing the cause proposed.

From the very nature of strictly secret marriages, the collection of information, of testimonies, and of documents, must be accomplished with the utmost secrecy, otherwise the investigation would eliminate the main characteristic of these marriages, namely secrecy. The method employed is quite divergent from that pursued in ordinary marriages, wherein the investigation must include the publishing of the proposed marriage. The paramount consideration, if the marriage is to be a Marriage of Conscience is secrecy. Such marriages are not ordinary but extraordinary. The law commands that these unions be entered secretly and with no announcements.[120] Whatever could tend to make public the fact of these marriages would have to be managed with the greatest discretion by the local Ordinary. As the sole judge of their necessity,[121] he is the legally responsible person in due maintenance of secrecy.

The general principle enunciated regarding the pastor's obligation to announce proposed marriages[122] suffers certain exceptions by the

[118] A complete exposition of what pre-nuptial investigation entails may be found in the recent Instruction of the Sacred Congregation of the Sacraments of June 29, 1941, which treats of this subject precisely.—*AAS, XXXIII* (1941), 291-308; *The Jurist,* II (1942) Supplement; for information on this matter before June 29, 1941, cf. Donovan, *The Pastor's Obligation in Pre-nuptial Investigation,* pp. 88-222.

[119] Donovan, *The Pastor's Obligation in Pre-nuptial Investigation,* p. 239; Reilly, *The General Norms of Dispensation,* p. 109.

[120] "Omissis denuntiationibus et secreto"—Canon 1104.

[121] Ayrinhac-Lydon, *Marriage Legislation,* p. 283.

[122] Canon 1022.

express permission of the law.[123] An exception of this kind obtains in regard to Marriages of Conscience,[124] in which the exception from the normal rule follows logically and necessarily from a consideration of the regulations that a public announcement of the proposed marriage is entirely out of place.[125] A separate dispensation from the banns, then, is not required, since it is contained in the permission given by the local Ordinary for the celebration of the marriage in question. Again, the fact that the law itself places the exception to the general requirement of announcing marriages is an indication that the Marriage of Conscience is an extraordinary form of marriage. As a result, in regard to the proper preparation and pre-nuptial investigation the Marriage of Conscience is not subject to the same kind of restrictions as other marriages, but proceeds under special regulations and implies the application of unique restrictions which do not obtain in relation to an ordinary marriage.

Article IV. Force of This Legislation

The final phrase of canon 1104 indicates that the method to be followed is that which is illustrated in the three canons immediately following. But before all consideration of the method itself, something must be determined concerning the effect occasioned for the type of marriage in question through the failure to observe the precise regulations. Previous to the Code the neglect to follow the prescribed form of secret registration certainly did not affect the valid character of the marriage,[126] nor are there any definite indications that carelessness or lack of regard for the enacted regulations regarding the registering of the marriage even rendered the celebration of such a marriage unlawful. If the requisite qualities were not present before or during the celebration of the marriage, for example, if the cause was not of sufficient gravity to warrant the permission of the Bishop, then the marriage was not canonically a Marriage of Conscience, and, in addition, in these instances, the marriage itself

123 Roberts, *The Banns of Marriage,* p. 94.

124 Canon 1104.

125 Roberts, *The Banns of Marriage,* p. 96.

126 *Supra,* p. 45.

was unlawful at least in the sense that it was entered in serious neglect of the special regulations given for Marriages of Conscience, or in contempt for the laws governing all marriages.

The illicitness of Marriages of Conscience may occur in the present in somewhat the same manner as previously. In the present law only the supreme ecclesiastical authority may authentically declare or constitute impediments of all kinds to marriage.[127] The failure to follow the requirements in Marriages of Conscience is not discovered among either the diriment or prohibitive impediments to marriage.[128] Therefore neglect or misuse of the regulations given for Marriages of Conscience would not render a Marriage of Conscience invalid, or even illicit in the sense that the neglect or misuse constituted a prohibitive impediment to licit marriage. The obvious interpretation of the canons dealing with this matter is that the exceptions granted in law and the special method indicated for Marriages of Conscience do not add to or subtract from the essentials of form, consent, and lack of impediments, which are necessary in every marriage.[129] However, now as formerly, because of the lack of sufficient cause or for other reasons permission to enter a Marriage of Conscience could be granted invalidly. In such an instance the marriage in question would revert to the state of an ordinary public marriage, and would be subject to all the laws regulating public marriages. If in spite of the invalid permission, a marriage progressed as a secret marriage employing the regulations and advantages offered for Marriages of Conscience, the marriage itself would be unlawful, because of the neglect to observe the requirements given in the law for public marriage.[130]

This chapter has been devoted to the discussion of the major elements involved in the granting of permission for a Marriage of Conscience. Local Ordinaries alone, to the exclusion of Vicars General not having a special mandate, are the competent superiors in

127 Canon 1038.

128 Cappello, *De Sacraments,* III, pars I, n. 205; Wernz-Vidal, *Ius Canonicum,* V, n. 149.

129 Canon 1081, 1; 1094.

130 Cf. canons 1020, 1024, 1097, 1; S. C. de Sacr., instr., 29 iun. 1941,—*AAS,* XXXIII (1941), 297-308.

their own territories. The cause presented by the parties must, after being verified, be found to combine in itself the notes of unusual gravity and extreme urgency. As in all marriages, it must be manifest to the proper superior that the parties are free to marry. The local Ordinary himself is not only competent, but also responsible, in all phases of the Marriage of Conscience already mentioned. The method to be invoked in completing all the details of a strictly secret marriage has been carefully enunciated in the Code. These instructions cover not only the immediate preparation for the marriage, but affect also the circumstances of the contract itself during the whole time of its existence as a Marriage of Conscience.

CHAPTER VII

THE PROMISE AND GRAVE OBLIGATION OF KEEPING THE FACT OF MARRIAGE SECRET

Canon 1105.—Permissio celebrationis matrimonii conscientiae secumfert promissionem et gravem obligationem secreti ex parte sacerdotis assistentis, testium, Ordinarii eiusque successorum, et etiam alterius coniugis, altero non consentiente divulgationi.

Article I. Nature of the Promise

Permission to contract a Marriage of Conscience brings with it the requirement of a promise of secrecy, and the grave obligation of preserving that promise. This promise is of the essence of the permission granted, since, if a marriage is to be a Marriage of Conscience, it must both in its celebration and duration remain unknown to the public.[1] Therefore, if the parties are unwilling to bind themselves in this manner, the permission for the marriage cannot be given to them.

A simple promise is a gratuitous and unilateral contract whereby the promisor binds himself to do something for the promisee. To become a contract in conscience, a promise must be accepted, and the acceptance must be manifested to the promisor.[2] The promise under consideration may best be designated as a mutual one, since it is assumed by several persons who promise identically, at least in regard to the maintenance of secrecy concerning the fact of marriage. Upon agreeing to keep the promise, and upon being given notice by the superior that the promise is accepted, all those involved become subject to a contract in conscience which becomes binding through the

[1] Wernz-Vidal, *Ius Canonicum,* V, n. 565.

[2] Noldin-Schmitt, *Summa Theologiae Moralis,* II, n. 546; Vermeersch, *Theologiae Moralis,* II, n. 405; Davis, *Moral and Pastoral Theology,* Heythrop Series, n. 2. (3. ed., 4 vols., London: Sheed and Ward, 1938), II, 365.

virtue of justice as well as that of fidelity,[3] because of the serious harm which would be done by those who would reveal the marriage without being released from the promise. Those who made the required promise may consider it accepted if they are allowed to continue in the capacity for the establishment of which the promises were originally proposed. Ultimate responsibility remains with the competent local Ordinary, who is presumed to accept the promise tended him if he offers no objection.

There are some indications that this promise may perhaps partake of the nature of a promissory oath.[4] Reputable authors require that before a Marriage of Conscience the parties faithfully promise to carry out the prescriptions of the law regarding the avoidance of scandal and the proper spiritual care of the children as mentioned in canon 1106.[5] These obligations, however, are incumbent only upon the parties and not on the witnesses, nor on the priest who assisted at the marriage, nor on the Ordinary. But all those who are mentioned in canon 1105 are held to the promise of keeping the marriage secret. Obviously the spouses are obligated principally and more extensively than the others involved. Their promise must necessarily differ in scope and, perhaps, in nature from that of the others. If the local Ordinary desires it, there is no reason for which he could not advise that the contracting parties take an oath concerning the points discussed in canon 1106, or at least recommend that they take an oath.[6] In fact, all concerned could be placed under a promissory oath binding as far as their respective obligations extended.[7]

From the words of the law, though, there is no demand for an oath. The law requires that all involved must make a serious promise to maintain secrecy, being fully cognizant of the grave nature of any

[3] Vermeersch, *Theologiae Moralis,* II, n. 406; Davis, *Moral and Pastoral Theology,* II, 365.

[4] Cf. canons 1318, 1319, 1320, for legislation concerning promissory oaths.

[5] "Coniuges debent *fidem interponere* se illas conditiones fideliter servaturos."—Wernz-Vidal, *Ius Canonicum,* V, n. 567; a similar requirement is posited in Cappello, *De Sacramentis,* III, pars II, n. 724.

[6] However, the local Ordinary could in no case force the taking of an oath, since oaths must be taken freely.—Canon 1317.

[7] Canon 1318.

infraction of that promise. The whole body of regulations in the Code of Canon Law concerning strictly secret marriages constitute a direct exception from the law.[8] They are employed in derogation from the general law by means of dispensation, and therefore they should be interpreted strictly.[9] The evident conclusion is that the words in canon 1105 which demand that a promise be taken cannot be extended of themselves to imply a requirement for an oath, since no such requirement is expressly indicated. Since the promise of secrecy is asked of all who know of these marriages, there arises the need to ascertain with some accuracy the nature of the secret assumed. It falls into the general classification of an entrusted or committed secret, which is one whose obligation arises from an agreement, arrived at antecedently to any disclosure, that the secret matter will be rigorously guarded.[10] Such a promise of secrecy may be either explicit or implicit, depending on whether the pledge to secrecy is asked for and received in so many words, or, though no pledge is asked for or received, the office or function of the person to whom the secret is committed clearly requires that the confidence imparted be sedulously guarded.[11] The professional or official secret has been described as a form of the implicit entrusted secret, because the secret is imparted, and the obligation of maintaining silence arises, precisely in view of the office or function its recipient exercises.[12]

In a Marriage of Conscience the promise of secrecy may be either explicit or implicit. The local Ordinary who grants the permission is bound to hold the secret of the marriage because of his office, and

[8] Cocchi, *Commentarium in Codicem Iuris Canonici* (8 vols., Taurinorum Augustae: Marietti, 1931-1940. Vol. I, 5. ed., 1938; Vol. II, 4. ed., 1937; Vol. III, 3. ed., 1931; Vol. IV, 3. ed., 1932; Vol. V, 5. ed., 1932; Vol. VI, 3. ed., 1933; Vol. VII, 3. ed., 1940; Vol. VIII, 4. ed., 1938), I, n. 121.

[9] Cf. Canon 19; Cicognani, *Canon Law,* (2. ed., Philadelphia: The Dolphin Press, 1935), p. 617.

[10] Noldin-Schmitt, *Summa Theologiae Moralis,* II, n. 666; Vermeersch, *Theologiae Moralis,* II, n. 647; Davis, *Moral and Pastoral Theology,* II, n. 392; Regan, *Professional Secrecy in the Light of Moral Principles,* (Washington, D. C.: Augustinian Press, 1943), p. 7.

[11] Regan, *Professional Secrecy in the Light of Moral Principles,* p. 8.

[12] Regan, *loc. cit.*

no express promise needs to be furnished by him. He is bound by an official secret.[13] The priest assisting, the contracting parties and the witnesses, should explicitly state their knowledge of the serious obligation to secrecy they are assuming. Upon mutually receiving this promise they are bound explicitly. Of course the local Ordinary may explicitly express his promise of secrecy if he wishes. On the other hand, in the words of the law there is no demand for an explicit promise from the priest, the parties and the witnesses, though in regard to these persons the requiring of an explicit promise would obviously reflect the safest and most satisfactory method. Marriages of Conscience are extraordinary affairs and, other than the local Ordinary, those who are involved can hardly be presumed to be acquainted with the exact nature of the obligations entailed, so that by reason of their official positions as persons necessary in the celebration of a Marriage of Conscience they would tender and receive the promise of secrecy implicitly.

An explicit promise or oath of secrecy, even if tendered and received by reason of one's office, at least in an individual case, cannot be classified with the usual professional or official promises or oaths of secrecy.[14] Such a promise simply connotes the presence of an explicit entrusted secret. The recommendation to require such an explicit promise of secrecy from all but the local Ordinary is not designed to place restrictions uncalled for in the law. The preservation of secrecy is of first importance if a marriage is to remain absolutely unknown to the public, and the promise of secrecy is required when permission to contract such a marriage is given. This promise of secrecy should be tendered and received on the part of those who are involved, in the way in which the law on this subject

[13] The canonical nature, extent, and additional examples of this type of secret are discussed in Hughes, *Witnesses in Criminal Trials of Clerics,* The Catholic University of America Canon Law Studies, n. 106 (Washington, D. C.: The Catholic University of America, 1937), p. 44; also in Król, *The Defendant in Contentious Trials,* The Catholic University of America Canon Law Studies, n. 146 (Washington, D. C.: The Catholic University of America Press, 1941), p. 119.

[14] Hogan, *Judicial Advocates and Procurators,* The Catholic University of America Canon Law Studies, n. 133 (Washington, D. C.: The Catholic University of America Press, 1941), p. 134; Król, *loc. cit.*

will best be fulfilled, and for this reason an explicitly committed promise is desired.

No one was expressly designated in the old law to receive the promises of secrecy concerning the fact of a Marriage of Conscience,[15] but the precedent was established that the superior who allowed the marriage also required a promise of some kind. In the present legislation this precedent has been adopted into the scope of the law. To the local Ordinary is reserved the knowledge and examination of the cause for the purpose of determining its gravity and necessity. He is obliged to personally assure himself of the character of the persons, and of their freedom for the contracting of the marriage.[16] Since the permission brings with it the promise of secrecy, the person executing that permission should take care that the implications of the permission are observed. The local Ordinary himself, then, in allowing a Marriage of Conscience, assumes the responsibility of seeing to it that the promises are properly tendered and received. There is no reason which precludes the receiving of these promises on the part of the priest who is to assist at the marriage, if they are submitted to the local Ordinary for scrutiny by that responsible authority before the ceremony. If this is not possible, the local Ordinary must at least have certain assurance that the promises of secrecy were properly executed before he accepts them. Since without acceptance the promises would not bind in conscience,[17] they must be made known to the local Ordinary before the ceremony, if they are to be regarded as validly tendered and received.

Substantially the promise of secrecy pledged by all concerned needs to regard only the strictly secret character of the marriage. Those involved must promise that they will not reveal the marriage as having taken place until they have been released from their promise of secrecy regarding the celebration of the marriage. The manner of release will be discussed in a subsequent chapter.

Canon 1105 does not indicate that the promises must be made in writing, nor is there any strict necessity for receiving them in this

[15] *Supra,* p. 53.

[16] Canon 1104; Cappello, *De Sacramentis,* III, pars II, n. 723; Wernz-Vidal, *Ius Canonicum,* V, n. 567.

[17] *Supra,* p. 88.

form. In a matter as serious as the present one, wherein the failure to keep the promise of secrecy would result in grave harm, the obligation to preserve it, whether it was made orally or in writing, derives from the virtue of justice.[18] However, certain advantages accrue to the use of some written form. Those involved would thus be enabled to acquire a clear and concise concept of the obligations they are assuming in pledging themselves to secrecy. The priest assisting at the marriage could expedite all the matters relevant to the celebration of the marriage with greater facility, and the superior allowing the marriage would have a definite idea of what was promised, together with proof of the facts that the promises were properly understood and tendered. Promises written and signed seem to reflect the most practicable method to be employed.

A. Gravity of the Obligation to Preserve Secrecy

Those who assume the obligation of preserving a promise of secrecy made by them as persons immediately connected with the execution of a permission to contract a Marriage of Conscience are held to regard that promise as binding gravely.[19] Whether the promise gives rise implicitly or explicitly to the guarding of an entrusted or committed secret, the moral obligation of guarding the secret is a most serious one, generally more serious than that which attaches to the natural or merely promised secret.[20] This is so because the entrusted secret involves an onerous contract binding in commutative justice.[21] Those species of entrusted secrets which are official secrets beget also an obligation in legal justice, because their observance is necessary for the common welfare.[22] Therefore, all those who fall under the obligation of maintaining secrecy regarding a Marriage of Conscience by reason of the promise they made in fulfilling the duty incumbent upon them, namely the local Ordinary, the assisting priest, the parties

[18] Vermeersch, *Theologia Moralis,* II, n. 406.

[19] Canon 1105.

[20] Noldin-Schmitt, *Summa Theologiae Moralis,* II, n. 669; Davis, *Moral and Pastoral Theology,* II, 424; Regan, *Professional Secrecy in the Light of Moral Principles,* p. 21.

[21] Noldin-Schmitt, *loc. cit.;* Regan, *loc. cit.*

[22] Noldin-Schmitt, *loc. cit;* Regan, *loc. cit.*

and the witnesses, are bound to keep their promise in view of a demand of commutative justice. The local Ordinary is in addition bound through legal justice, if the observance of the secret is required of him for the proper safeguarding of the public welfare.

If in the granting of permission for a Marriage of Conscience the local Ordinary is in fact also the Bishop of the diocese, he becomes by his act subject to an obligation which derives from the demand inherent in the keeping of an official secret.[23] A Bishop has

[23] If one abstracts from the consideration of the Sacramental secret, and of other forms of secrets which fall within the scope of the forum of conscience, inclusive of both the sacramental and extra-sacramental, there are four canonical types of secret regarding which legislation is contained in the Code of Canon Law. All four share the common essence of being entrusted or committed secrets, but each embodies in itself individuating characteristics which relate to the specific cases wherewith the secret has to deal.

1.) The official secret binds by reason of the office possessed by the person to whom the secret is confided. With the exception of the Bishop, all who are constituted as members of the diocesan tribunal must take an oath that they will faithfully and efficiently fulfill the trust committed to them,—Canon 1621. In certain cases the correct fulfillment of their oath requires strict secrecy on their part regarding the proceedings,—Canons 1623, 1625, § 2, § 3. The Code does not require a new or additional oath of secrecy for holding such persons to the obligation of preserving secrecy, since they are already held by their oath of office, which in its observance requires secrecy whenever it is so commanded by law. Such secrets are implicitly entrusted secrets. The official secret differs from the sworn secret. Cf. Król, *The Defendant in Contentious Trials,* p. 118; Moriarty, *Oaths in Ecclesiastical Courts,* The Catholic University of America Canon Law Studies, n. 110 (Washington, D. C.: The Catholic University of America, 1937), p. 59.

2.) Sworn secrecy is occasioned by the imposition of an oath of secrecy in certain cases in which the judge deems it wise and prudent,—Canons 1623, § 3; 1769; Król, *op. cit.,* p. 119; Moriarty, *loc. cit.* These oaths of secrecy are administered in specific circumstances, and in separate cases. They are not automatically binding as is the official secret. These secrets whose keeping is strengthened and confirmed by oaths are explicitly entrusted secrets.

3.) Professional secrecy binds certain persons to whom a secret has been committed for the purpose of seeking counsel.—Canon 1755, § 2, 1°; Hughes, *Witnesses in Criminal Trials of Clerics,* p. 44. Such persons are

already, at the time of his consecration, taken an oath which embraces the promise to fulfill his office to the best of his ability,[24] and if the most perfect manner of fulfilling his office entails the maintenance of strict secrecy in accomplishing a given task committed to him by the common law, no new oath is demanded of him.[25] In Marriages of Conscience no new oath of secrecy at all is demanded of anyone at the time the permission for the contraction of such a marriage is given, but the local Ordinary in the very act of granting this permission would be acting in fulfillment of the oath taken by him at the time of his consecration, namely, the oath to follow the prescriptions of the common law which bind him to official secrecy.

The promise to secrecy made by all others than the local Or-

bound because of the confidential nature of the information received in their daily professional occupations. No ecclesiastically administered oath binds them to secrecy. Knowledge held in professional secrecy constitutes an implicitly entrusted secret.

4.) The promise of secrecy made by persons, who, not inclusive of the Bishop, fulfill some capacity in a Marriage of Conscience differs from all the above mentioned secrets. Its nature is explained in the text of the present study.

Some moral theologians make no clear distinctions between the various types of entrusted secrets. The official secret includes the professional secret, while the sworn secret is simply one that is promised privately. Cf. Noldin-Schmitt, *Summa Theologiae Moralis,* II, n. 666; Vermeersch, *Theologiae Moralis,* II, n. 647; Davis, *Moral and Pastoral Theology,* II, 423. However, Regan (*Professional Secrecy in the Light of Moral Principles,* p. 49) states that there are members of society who are bound to secrecy more strictly than those bound merely by professional secrecy. These include the officials of the Roman Curia. They are bound also to official secrecy, of which professional secrecy is then a subdivision. Thus the canonical division is hinted at, though definite distinctions between the four types of secrets are not supplied in the manner here outlined.

24 Cocchi, *Commentarium in Codicem Iuris Canonici,* IV, n. 41; Vermeersch-Creusen, *Epitome,* III, n. 63.

25 Bishops who themselves exercise judiciary power are excepted from all obligation of taking an oath rightly to fulfill their office in the tribunal. (Canon 1621, § 1.) But if they act as judge in the cases mentioned in canon 1623 they certainly are held to the obligation of a strict official secrecy.

dinary is not of an official character in the canonical sense, since no oath of office accompanies it to bestow upon it an official character. Ordinarily the promise is made explicitly and not merely implicitly. As with sworn secrets so the secrets of these persons are pledged explicitly, on the other hand, these secrets differ from sworn secrets, since in the promises made in preparation for Marriages of Conscience no oath is demanded as in sworn secrets. The obligation to preserve the required secrecy in respect of the Marriages of Conscience binds in somewhat the same manner as the obligation which is inherent in professional secrets, though the keeping of the latter secrets binds implicitly, while the keeping of the former binds explicitly. Therefore, in the cases which form the subject of this work the promise of secrecy has unique characteristics, in that it is pledged mutually by all who are involved; it is assumed as an obligation explicitly in the ordinary course of events, and by means of a serious obligation in conscience it binds every person who made the promise.[26]

Most of the regulations supplied in the legislation on Marriages of Conscience in the Code of Canon Law are extraordinary, for they entail a general deviation from the usual method of arranging and performing marriages. The required promise of secrecy is no exception. It does not fit easily into any but the most general divisions of the promises of secrecy. A special division may be reserved for it, or it may be considered simply as an entrusted secret with special applications. Regardless of the specific classification to which it is assigned, however, and in addition to the general serious culpability attached to all violation of entrusted secrets, the law implies a grave obligation to preserve the pledged secret on the part of all to whose knowledge the secret has come in the arrangement for the particular Marriage of Conscience in question.[27]

At times the keeping of an entrusted secret may be confirmed with an oath. If, on the advice of the local Ordinary, the parties involved assume their obligation with a sworn promise of secrecy,

[26] Such a promise of secrecy always binds in justice under pain of mortal sin.—Noldin-Schmitt, *Summa Theologiae Moralis,* II, n. 669; Vermeersch, *Theologiae Moralis,* II, n. 648; Davis, *Moral and Pastoral Theology,* II, 424.

[27] Canon 1105.

this added circumstance does not change the nature or the conditions inherent in the secret which must be kept. The oath remains as something accessory and therefore does not substantially modify the nature of the principal, namely the secret, as it is in itself.[28] Thus, if some just cause demands that the secret fact of marriage be revealed by those who are competent to do so, a promissory oath would not stand in the way of divulgation, or make it necessary to have a more serious cause to reveal the marriage.[29] It is important to note, however, that the taking of an oath, provided the conditions for a valid and licit oath are realized, will add another species of obligation to that of the secret itself, so that the violation of an entrusted or committed secret whose keeping is strengthened and confirmed by an oath entails an offense against the virtue of religion, as well as the virtue of justice.[30]

B. Instruction to be Given to the Contracting Parties Before the Marriage

An obligation exists for the pastor to satisfy himself, in every case, that the parties to a proposed Christian marriage are sufficiently instructed.[31] He is to supply instruction in every instance in which he deems it necessary. Particular attention is to be given to assuring himself that the parties contemplating marriage have adequate knowledge concerning the sanctity and indissolubility of marriage, as well as a true realization of their obligations towards each other and towards their children.[32] No permission is granted anywhere in the law whereby the local Ordinary or the pastor assisting at a Marriage of Conscience may feel not to be obligated to pursue the course indicated in the common law regarding this pre-nuptial instruction.

[28] Canon 1318, 1.

[29] Coronata, *Institutiones Iuris Canonici* (5 vols., Taurini Romae: Marietti, 1933-1939. Vols. I-II, 2 ed., 1939; Vol. III, 1933; Vol. IV, 1935; Vol. V, 1936), II, n. 902.

[30] Regan, *Professional Secrecy in the Light of Moral Principles,* p. 10.

[31] Pius XI, encycl. *Casti connubii,* 31 dec. 1930—*AAS,* XXII (1931), 539.

[32] Canon 1033; S. C. de Sacr., instr. 29 iun. 1941, § 8—*AAS,* XXXIII (1941), 302; *The Jurist,* II (1942), Supplement, p. 6.

Their responsibility is not only present in these as in all other marriages, but, because of the special circumstances surrounding Marriages of Conscience, those who arrange them must give added instructions to make certain that the parties to the marriage understand thoroughly the obligations incumbent upon them as persons entering a Marriage of Conscience, which added instruction would not be demanded for them as persons entering an ordinary public marriage. The contracting parties, therefore, must be admonished to forestall all scandal, to have their progeny baptized in the manner prescribed, and to rear their children as catholics in accord with the demands of canon 1106.[33]

No explicit requirement has been enacted in the Code of Canon Law in consequence of which either an additional admonition or a wider instruction must be given to the parties of a Marriage of Conscience. The requirement of this admonition is postulated by the nature of the method inherent in the celebration of these marriages, and by the impossibility of conscientious observance of the enactments of the law in the absence of such an admonition. If the parties are to be bound by unusual regulations, they must know of them before they can be bound by them. Again, if the superior who has permitted the marriage may reveal its celebration in certain cases, the parties must know in what circumstances their marriage may rightfully be divulged by the competent authority. Otherwise they could hardly be expected to avoid the occasioning of such circumstances.

There is no doubt at all that it was the wish of Benedict XIV to have the parties of these marriages advised concerning their obligations before the ceremony.[34] Therefore, from the time of the

[33] Ayrinhac-Lydon, *Marriage Legislation,* p. 284. The obligations of the parties towards each other and towards their children in the light of the peculiar regulations affecting Marriages of Conscience are treated in the following chapter.

[34] "Uni tamen, aut alteri Sacramenti Ministro a Vobis deputando districte praecipiatur, ne Matrimonio intersit, nisi prius paterna caritate Coniuges in Domino monuerit, Sobolem procreandam regenerar quamprimum oportere sacro Baptismatis lavacro; ac Christo Iudici districtam reddituros esse rationem, nisi filios ut legitimos agnoverint, eosque pietate, bonisque moribus imbuerint, et frui patienter bonis temporalibus, a Maiori-

establishment of the external forum Marriage of Conscience till the time of the present Code of Canon Law, there was an explicit command to administer an admonition before the marriage. Though this is not required in so many words in the present legislation, a valid interpretation in accord with the context of the law recognizes the demand for an admonition, since not the entire set of regulations regarding Marriages of Conscience can or will properly be applied in the absence of such an admonition.[35]

Modern authors not only understand an admonition to be necessary, but also have widened the scope of the admonition to include a prenuptial promise regarding the intention the spouses must have for observing the regulations concerning the avoidance of scandal, and the procuring of the baptism and religious education of the children.[36] The foundation for this demand is again the fact that the parties ought to give their word that they will not force the use of the powers of divulgation reserved to ecclesiastical authorities by manifesting disobedience to the requirements of the law in their case.[37] The request for such guarantees extends only to the parties of the Marriage of Conscience. As is obvious from their nature, these additional promises or assurances are not to be made by nor do they bind the witnesses, the assisting priest or the local Ordinary. The making of these promises is not demanded in the present, nor was it demanded in the previous legislation. Certainly the giving of these promises would prove helpful on the part of the spouses in acquiring a better understanding and keener realization of their obligations. The local Ordinary moreover could feel more assured of

bus in supremis tabulis relictis, vel provida legum auctoritate delatis.—Ep. encycl. *Satis Vobis,* 17 nov. 1741, § 9, § 13, § 14—*Fontes,* n. 319.

[35] Canon 18.

[36] Cappello, *De Sacramentis,* III, pars II, n. 724; Wernz-Vidal, *Ius Canonicum,* V, n. 569. Payen (*De Matrimonio,* II, n. 1942) simply demands the giving of the admonition. He notes, without comment, that other authors also demand a promise regarding the fulfillment of the mentioned obligation. He does not state his own opinion.

[37] "In omnibus hisce casibus Ecclesia sibi reservat ius matrimonium secreto celebratum publicandi, et idcirco antequam ad talem secretam celebrationem procedatur coniuges debent fidem interponere se illas conditiones fideliter servaturos."—Wernz-Vidal, *Ius Canonicum,* V, n. 569.

having efficiently and faithfully fulfilled his duty, if these guarantees were received by him.

The local Ordinary, therefore, has an obligation to admonish the contracting parties of the special obligations attendant upon their entering a Marriage of Conscience. He may likewise urge the parties to promise or take an oath that they will observe the duties they accept in being given permission to contract a Marriage of Conscience. These promises or oaths would best be made in writing, and could then be conveniently attached to, and preserved with, the promise of secrecy which must be made by the parties.

Article II. Those Bound by the Promise

Those who are bound to preserve the promise of secrecy made before a Marriage of Conscience is entered into are the local Ordinary and his successors, the priest assisting, the parties themselves, and the witnesses of the marriage.[38] Both parties may agree to divulge the existence of their marriage and, for specific reasons, the local Ordinary may also reveal that fact.[39] But no exceptions other than these are provided for in the law. Therefore, an intentional revelation of the fact of a strictly secret marriage by any of the other parties involved in the arrangements preceding it would constitute a mortal sin for the guilty person.[40]

From a moral viewpoint it must be remembered that all who are held by the promise of secrecy are bound by a mutual contractual obligation. In such cases the consent, or desire, of one member for the revelation of the secret is not sufficient.[41] In the case at hand, the consent of one of the parties to the marriage would not furnish adequate grounds for revealing a Marriage of Conscience. Again, presumed consent is not easily justified as a liberative factor when the secret is shared mutually and must be honored as an explicitly entrusted secret for in such instances there is a question of a contractual duty, and the assent of the other party to the manifesta-

38 Canon 1105.

39 Canons 1105, 1106.

40 Petrovits, *The New Church Law on Matrimony,* p. 369.

41 Regan, *Professional Secrecy in the Light of Moral Principles,* p. 100.

tion, similarly as in actions placed against common agreements, is not presumed.[42]

The exemption which is enjoyed in an ecclesiastical court by those who are bound by a professional secret could also be employed in favor of those who are obliged to keep a Marriage of Conscience secret.[43] Likewise, it would not be necessary for such persons to divulge their entrusted secret in a civil court.[44]

Practically, if the assisting priest or the witnesses are of the well-founded opinion that the parties of a Marriage of Conscience no longer deserve the consideration of the Church in keeping their marriage secret, or if they have discovered circumstances which indicate that a divulgation of the marriage seems advisable, then, lacking the mutual and actual agreement of the parties to reveal the marriage, they should inform the local Ordinary who originally permitted the marriage. Other than the parties themselves, he alone may reveal the marriage in the cases mentioned in the law. If the presented facts seem to necessitate, or to counsel the exposing of the fact of the marriage, the person in whose favor the exceptions in the law have been established, namely the local Ordinary, is the judge of whether resort should be made to actual revelation. It would be difficult to suppose a case in which such grave danger impends that the priest or the witnesses would find it necessary to reveal the marriage to avert a serious harm, there not being sufficient time to inform the local Ordinary beforehand. However, for an extremely grave reason these persons would be excused from ob-

[42] Regan, *Loc. cit.*

[43] Canon 1755, § 1, 1°. Persons enjoying the exemption which is extended to those who are bound by professional secrecy may testify if a.) they are released from the bond of secrecy by the interested parties, and b.) they prudently feel they can testify. Both factors must coexist.—S. C. de Sacr., instr. *Provida Mater,* 15 aug. 1936, art. 121, 1, 1—*AAS,* XXVIII (1936), 312-370; Bouscaren, *Canon Law Digest,* II, 233; Doheny, *Canonical Procedure in Matrimonial Cases* (Milwaukee: The Bruce Publishing Company, 1938), p. 232. If both parties have consented to the divulgation of their secret marriage, then all who were held by a promise of secrecy can testify to its existence, but only if they consider that it is the part of prudence to do so.

[44] Woywod, *Practical Commentary on the Code,* II, 268.

serving their promise of secrecy.[45] Though none but the local Ordinary and the parties of the marriage may divulge it, if others through culpable imprudence do reveal it, and the knowledge of the marriage really becomes public, the marriage must then be treated as a public marriage and the recording of it must be entered with the ordinary marriage records.[46]

The question of whether others who may come to know of a strictly secret marriage are bound to observe secrecy is quite simply solved. The secret involved is an entrusted one. In accord with the principles of moral theology, no one may unjustly attempt to explore, manifest, or use another's secret.[47] To do so would involve the commission of a serious sin against the virtue of justice. Even if knowledge of the secret were justly acquired, such information could not be manifested or used, as long as the original possessor of the committed secret did not consent to it.[48] If persons other than those mentioned in canon 1105 discover that a Marriage of Conscience has taken place, or is to be celebrated, they are bound to maintain strict silence regarding this fact, and consequently may not use such knowledge to their own or another's advantage.

The parties of a marriage of this kind can certainly be presumed to be unwilling to have the fact of their marriage published, else they would not have entered it secretly in the first place. The law demands a promise of secrecy which is accompanied with a grave obligation to maintain the secret from all those who are immediately concerned with the Marriage of Conscience. It is in keeping with this law, designed carefully to secure secrecy, that others who know of such a marriage must refrain from manifesting it. From a correct interpretation of the law and of the common principles of moral theology it follows that, if outside persons obtain knowl-

[45] Petrovits, *The New Church Law on Matrimony,* p. 369.

[46] Cappello, *De Sacramentis,* III, pars II, n. 724.

[47] Noldin-Schmitt, *Summa Theologiae Moralis,* II, n. 666.

[48] Noldin-Schmitt, *loc. cit.;* Vermeersch, *Theologia Moralis,* II, n. 649; Davis, *Moral and Pastoral Theology,* II, 424; Regan, *Professional Secrecy in the Light of Moral Principles,* p. 21.

edge of a strictly secret marriage,[40] they are forbidden to make the marriage known apart from the consent of the parties.[50]

A. The Priest Assisting

The law does not prescribe who is to be the priest assisting at a Marriage of Conscience. Those competent by law to assist at marriages include the local Ordinary of the parties, their pastor, or the delegate of either local Ordinary or the pastor.[51] In the case of a strictly secret marriage the priest assisting must be a competent one.[52] There is no conflict between the competence required in ordinary marriages and in Marriages of Conscience. Naturally, since only the local Ordinary himself may allow the latter marriages, the priest who assists at such marriages must know that the requisite permission has been granted. Normally he would not know of it until he has been designated to assist at the marriage, unless he presented the case to the local Ordinary himself. In addition, then to the competence required for assistance at a public marriage the only other quality necessarily demanded in ministers assisting at Marriages of Conscience is their designation by the local Ordinary. Once commissioned to assist at a marriage of this kind, it certainly would not be in keeping with the spirit of the law to delegate another priest. Such a manner of proceeding would, without warrant, extend knowledge of the proposed marriage, which knowledge the law desires to be closely guarded.

The local Ordinary himself is of course competent to assist at the marriage of his subjects.[53] If he so desired, then, he could both grant the needed permission for a Marriage of Conscience and also

40 Regarding the question of the revelation of the marriage it would make no difference whether knowledge of the fact of the marriage was acquired justly or unjustly. It matters not whether the information was obtained simply by chance or through the exercise of a culpable curiosity. In either case the obligation to observe continued secrecy remains the same.—Noldin-Schmitt, *loc. cit.*

50 Woywod, *Practical Commentary on the Code,* I, 696.

51 Canon 1094.

52 Vermeersch-Creusen, *Epitome,* II, n. 410.

53 Canon 1094.

personally assist at the marriage. This method is to be recommended, if it does not prove inconvenient, since it would reduce the number of those who would know of the marriage. The old law strongly encouraged the deputation of one of the pastors of the parties to assist at a Marriage of Conscience as the acceptable method.[54] Those pastors had, as pastors still have in the present, the advantage of knowing one or both of the persons involved, and ordinarily were possessed of a diversified pastoral experience to recommend them. None the less, if the circumstances of the case seemed to demand the use of a priest other than one of the pastors, the Bishop, for a grave and impelling cause then, was to select a priest who by his probity, knowledge and skill exhibited himself as capable of executing the commission to arrange for and to assist at the particular Marriage of Conscience in question.[55]

With the present law lacking any explicit determination, the prescriptions of the previous legislation on the same subject are to be invoked to obtain direction.[56] In the present, therefore, two points should be observed by the local Ordinary when he grants permission for Marriages of Conscience, in regard to the designation of a competent priest to assist at the ceremony. First, those who, other than the local Ordinary himself, possess the primary right of witnessing these marriages are the pastors of the parties who by reason of their parochial office are fully competent. Secondly, a grave cause is required before another priest may be designated. Even then not simply any other priest may be selected, but one who is endowed with special qualities of knowledge and experience.[57]

[54] Benedictus XIV, ep. encycl. *Satis Vobis,* 17 nov. 1741, § 8—*Fontes,* n. 319.

[55] Benedictus XIV, *loc. cit.*

[56] Canon 6, 2.

[57] The exact nature of the grave cause here required and carried over from the old law is nowhere detailed. Since these marriages are essentially secret, any set of circumstances wherein the designation of the pastor as the celebrant would endanger the secret character of the union, appears to furnish a grave enough cause to permit the local Ordinary to commission another priest as the celebrant. Such a grave cause could be considered as present, for instance, if the pastor of the parties is violently and unjustly opposed to their secret marriage, or if he is

B. The Witnesses

At least the qualities desired of witnesses for ordinary marriages [58] ought to be present in witnesses of a Marriage of Conscience. Benedict XIV demanded that a greater diligence be exercised in the selection of persons who were to be witnesses of a strictly secret marriage than in the cases of ordinary marriage. His recommendation was that trustworthy persons were to be used, so that no knowledge or rumor of the marriage would arise.[59] In the absence of explicit requirements in the present law, one may again look to the classic document of the old law on the subject under discussion for a correct interpretation,[60] since the present regulations were developed from those which were established in the *Satis Vobis*. Local Ordinaries, therefore, still have the obligation, as formerly, of exercising sedulous care in selecting the witnesses for Marriages of Conscience.[61]

The group of persons who are best acquainted with the nature of secret marriages, their characteristics, and their attendant obligations, are priests. Whenever it is possible priests should be named as witnesses then, since the celebration and the continuation of the marriage in secrecy could be most satisfactorily accomplished by following this method. If other persons are employed as witnesses they should be informed of the nature of their duties, and should never be accepted as witnesses to a proposed secret marriage unless their reputation indicates their trustworthiness and their conscientious capacity for keeping the promise of secrecy to which they are subject.

C. The Ordinary and His Successors

The Ordinary here spoken of is understood to be the local Ordinary who originally permitted the Marriage of Conscience. The

related to the parties and in consequence thereof has the misguided impression that they are already validly married.

58 Cappello, *De Sacramentis,* III, pars II, n. 653; Vermeersch-Creusen, *Epitome,* II, n. 397; Wernz-Vidal, *Ius Canonicum,* V, n. 540.

59 Ep. encycl. *Satis Vobis,* 17 nov. 1741, § 6—*Fontes,* n. 319.

60 Canon 6, 2°.

61 Vermeersch-Creusen, *Epitome,* II, n. 410.

question of the competence of the local Ordinary has already been discussed in some detail,[62] and it has likewise been indicated who are the lawful successors of local Ordinaries.[63] All these are bound to observe the promise of secrecy when they have made it. Residential Bishops would of necessity come to a knowledge of the Marriages of Conscience contracted in their territory during the incumbency of their predecessors, because they are the lawful custodians and sole inspectors of the diocesan Secret Archives, wherein these marriages are registered, and wherein any newly supplied information in their regard is preserved.[64]

There is no reason for a successor to a Vicar General to know of the Marriages of Conscience for the contraction of which his predecessor gave the requisite permissions in virtue of the special mandate committed to him. The new entries concerning these marriages are made by the Bishop Ordinary. The Vicar General has no personal legal right to inspect the secret archives of the diocese.[65]

D. *The Parties to the Marriage*

The obligation of secrecy which is assumed by all concerned is asserted in the law in favor of the parties to a Marriage of Conscience.[66] If both parties consent to have their marriage made known, then the obligation of secrecy imposed by the law on all the persons mentioned in canon 1105 ceases. However, in accord with the words of the law the consent of one party for the divulgation of the marriage would in no way affect the obligation of secrecy which binds all the persons involved. Each of the contracting parties is entitled to the right to have his or her marriage remain secret, and the express, joint permission of both parties is required before the marriage may be revealed by either of the consorts.[67]

So emphatic are the words of the Code of Canon Law on this point, that the presumed or tacit permission of the second party

[62] *Supra,* pp. 58-61.

[63] *Supra,* p. 62.

[64] Canon 379, § 4; Louis, *Diocesan Archives,* p. 82.

[65] Louis, *Diocesan Archives,* p. 83.

[66] Woywod, *Practical Commentary on the Code,* I, 696.

[67] Petrovits, *The New Church Law on Matrimony,* p. 369.

would not suffice to justify the divulgation which the first party desires to effect. In the absence of express consent of both parties neither of the parties is absolved from the obligation of preserving secrecy. To disregard this obligation would imply the guilt of a serious fault, the guilt consisting in this that, contrary to the promise, there is an intentional communication of knowledge to others regarding the secret character of the marriage.[68]

In cases wherein the parties mutually agree to reveal their marriage, reverence and a sense of duty would indicate that they inform the local Ordinary of their intention. He should certainly in some way know of their action in order that as a result of it neither he nor the others will any longer feel bound by the regulations regarding strictly secret marriages. He should know of it furthermore in order that their marriage and the baptisms of their children may be entered in the ordinary parish registers.[69]

68 Petrovits, *loc. cit.*
69 Wernz-Vidal, *Ius Canonicum,* V, n. 570.

CHAPTER VIII

RELAXATION OF THE OBLIGATION TO PRESERVE SECRECY

Canon 1106.—Huius promissionis obligatio ex parte Ordinarii non extenditur ad casum quo vel aliquod scandalum aut gravis erga matrimonii sanctitatem iniuria ex secreti observantia immineat, vel parentes non curent filios ex tali matrimonio susceptos baptizari aut eos baptizandos curent falsis expressis nominibus, quin interim Ordinario intra triginta dies notitiam prolis susceptae et baptizatae cum sincera indicatione parentum praebeant, vel christianam filiorum educationem negligant.

Article I. Nature of the Power of the Local Ordinary in These Cases

In the present law the obligation of preserving secrecy on the part of the local Ordinary and the spouses is conditional.[1] The parties to the marriage may divulge their secret marriage in consequence of a common agreement between themselves,[2] and the local Ordinary who permitted the marriage bears no continued obligation of preserving secrecy in the cases mentioned in canon 1106. In the old law those who flagrantly disobeyed or exhibited disrespect for the regulations to be followed both for the celebration and also the duration of the Marriages of Conscience were to be proportionately punished.[3] In cases wherein human respect led the parties to be

[1] Cappello, *De Sacramentis,* III, pars II, n. 724; Payen, *De Matrimonio, II,* n. 1946.

[2] Canon 1105.

[3] "Quia vero nonnulli deesse non possunt, qui propriae conscientiae vocibus obsurdescant, et nostris hisce mandatis parere negligant; debita poenarum districtione pro modo culpae a Vobis puniantur."—Benedictus XIV, ep. encycl. *Satis Vobis,* 17 nov. 1741, § 12—*Fontes,* n. 319.

tardy in reporting the baptism of their offspring beyond the time limit set by the law the parties were to suffer divulgation of their secret marriage.[4]

In the law as it exists at the present time no formal punishment is threatened or sanctioned. The punishments proposed in the old law have not survived in the new, and therefore they cannot be applied.[5] Likewise, there is no specification in the present law that, when one or more of the circumstances described in canon 1106 are verified, the Marriage of Conscience must be divulged by the local Ordinary.[6] In the words of the law itself, the obligation of the local Ordinary of preserving secrecy concerning the fact of marriage simply does not extend to, or exist, in certain cases. Therefore, when one of these situations is verified, then with respect to the local Ordinary the right of the parties to have the originally secret character of their marriage respected and guarded is forfeited. It is to be understood in every case from the very beginning, that the permission to enter a Marriage of Conscience, and the subsequent promise of secrecy, are not absolute. As far as the local Ordinary is concerned, this permission and promise never comprehend or include the cases mentioned in canon 1106.

The tenor of this canon indicates that the law at present is somewhat different from what it was formerly, so that when the preservation of secrecy ceases to bind the local Ordinary he may make the fact of marriage public, but is not compelled to do so. If he prudently feels the situation can be rectified by his interviewing the parties and cautioning them regarding his intention to reveal the marriage if the circumstances which they have occasioned are not rectified in accord with the original agreement he made with them,

4 Benedictus XIV, *loc. cit.*

5 Canon 6, 5°.

6 Petrovits (*The New Church Law on Matrimony,* p. 29) asserts the local Ordinary is free "to make the marriage public by way of punishment imposed on the parties for the neglect of their duties". In accord with the words of the law the local Ordinary may divulge the marriage, but there is no indication that this constitutes a punishment. If it were a punishment it would be interesting to know as what type of punishment it could be classified since it does not fit easily into any of the categories of punishments mentioned in the Code.

he can still continue to preserve secrecy. The faculty remaining with the local Ordinary of divulging the marriage is no longer of a specifically penal nature, but is given to protect the common good, the dignity of the sacrament, and the status of the children of strictly secret marriages, rather than to punish the parties to the marriage. In fact, there are cases in which the marriage should be manifested even when both parties are in no manner formally guilty, and therefore merit no punishment.[7]

When the local Ordinary finds himself absolved from preserving secrecy, and is of the opinion that the continuation of secrecy would be harmful, his obligations of ruling his diocese according to the norms of canon law[8] revert to him, and, as a consequence, he must see to it that the marriage and the baptisms of the children of the marriage in question are registered in the ordinary parochial registers as is done for marriages which are public from the beginning.[9] Having decided to reveal the marriage he should also inform the witnesses and the parties of the marriage themselves that the marriage is no longer to be regarded as a Marriage of Conscience, but as an ordinary public marriage.

The enumeration of the cases listed in canon 1106 is of an exclusive character. This is true because the whole body of regulations found in the law concerning strictly secret marriage constitutes a direct exception from the law,[10] and, therefore, must be interpreted strictly.[11] Though the list is factually exhaustive, however, the cases constituting it are general enough to embrace many specific instances in which the obligation of secrecy on the part of the local Ordinary would cease to bind. None the less, given a case which would not fit into the specifications for the established cases of canon 1106,

[7] This could occur when grave scandal is given though every precaution to avoid it has been employed. Again, in instances wherein one of the parties is unfaithful to the marriage it may be revealed to protect the dignity of the Sacrament. However, there is no reason to construe this revelation as a punishment meted out against an innocent party in either case.

[8] Canons 335, § 1; 336, § 1.

[9] Canons 1103; 777.

[10] Cocchi, *Commentarium in Codicem Iuris Canonici,* I, n. 121.

[11] Canon 19; Cicognani, *Canon Law,* p. 617.

the local Ordinary cannot feel that his obligation to preserve secrecy has ceased. He may request the parties to reveal their marriage in this instance, but he could not force them to do so.

The obligation of preserving secrecy ceases to bind the local Ordinary in five instances:

1. When scandal threatens from continued observance of the secret;
2. When a grave injury to the sanctity of marriage has become imminent;
3. When the parents of children born to a Marriage of Conscience neglect to have their offspring baptized;
4. When the parents have the children baptized, under false names, but fail to report the facts of birth and of baptism to the local Ordinary within thirty days with a true indication of the parentage;
5. When parents neglect the Christian education of their children.

Each of these cases will be discussed in the order in which they occur in the law, and as here stated.

Article II. The Question of Scandal

Active scandal is a word or an act evil in itself, or at least having the appearance of evil, which is the occasion of another's sin.[12] Its mention in canon 1106 as a factor which liberates the local Ordinary from his continued obligation to preserve secrecy is not the only place in the law wherein scandal is recognized as seriously hampering the use of an extraordinary power of dispensation granted by the common law to local Ordinaries.[13] The purpose of the relaxation of

[12] Noldin-Schmitt, *Summa Theologiae Moralis,* II, n. 102; Vermeersch, *Theologiae Moralis,* II, n. 111; Davis, *Moral and Pastoral Theology,* I, 333.

[13] The faculties granted in canon 1043 may be employed only *"remoto scandalo"*. Scandal is likewise a powerful factor in estimating the gravity of penalties to be imposed, and merits such immediate attention in some instances that when it is present punishment may be imposed without any previous warning at all. Cf. canons 2218, § 1; 2222. The purpose in adducing these examples is to demonstrate that scandal usually constitutes a circumstance gravely affecting the advantages offered in the law.

the obligation of secrecy in the cases under discussion is to remove for the good of the faithful all the occasions of sin incidental to the attendant scandal.[14]

The parties of a strictly secret marriage, being joined by a valid union which is a sacrament, know themselves privileged to participate in and enjoy all the acts pertinent to ordinary married life. However, the faithful, being completely ignorant of the married status of such persons, could readily take scandal from their actions. Therefore the display of an intimate familiarity between the parties which has become the subject of public comment would constitute and nourish the scandal spoken of in canon 1106.[15] Not only to preserve the marriage in secrecy, therefore, but also to avoid any infraction of the divine law of charity, those who are united in a Marriage of Conscience must conduct themselves in public in such a manner that they do not offer an occasion of scandal to others.[16]

Scandal occurring in the manner above described would ordinarily have to be considered as an actively given scandal, for the parties know of their obligation to refrain from acting in public as married persons and thereby being the occasion of another's sin,[17] in spite of the fact that in consequence of their valid union no sinfulness would inherently attach to the acts performed or the words exchanged by them. Those who live in a Marriage of Conscience cannot upon giving scandal be excused by means of the applied principle of the twofold effect, whereby the enjoyment of their marital rights could be considered as the good effect directly and actively intended, but the publicly offered occasion of sin as the evil effect

[14] Payen, *De Matrimonio,* II, n. 1947.

[15] Payen, *loc. cit.* Scandal might also occur in cases wherein the parties to a Marriage of Conscience, which had been entered to remedy concubinage, would separate. Not the manner of the occurrence of scandal, therefore, but the fact of scandal constitutes the situation in which the local Ordinary may feel free to divulge the marriage.

[16] Cappello, *De Sacramentis,* III, pars II, n. 725; Wernz-Vidal, *Ius Canonicum,* V, n. 568; Woywod, *Practical Commentary on the Code,* I, 697.

[17] Genicot-Salsmans, *Institutiones Theologiae Moralis* (14 ed., 2 vols., Buenos Aires: Dedebeç Ediciones Desclée, De Brouwer, 1939), I, 178; Noldin-Schmitt, *Summa Theologiae Moralis,* II, n. 103; Davis, *Moral and Pastoral Theology,* II, 333.

which is not directly intended but only passively sustained or tolerated. The principle, though morally sound,[18] can find no place in any application of law which would result in a direct contradiction of the regulations sanctioned by the divine law in its absolute interdiction of scandal. The regulation against scandal as enacted in canon 1106 intends principally to safeguard the good of the faithful, but this intent could not be accomplished if, in a given case of scandal, the advantages offered to the two persons living in a Marriage of Conscience were to be preferred to the common good.

Before the Code of Canon Law when scandal was occasioned by a Marriage of Conscience it was considered as received and not given actively.[19] However, no explicit mention of scandal as a factor liberating the local Ordinary from secrecy is discovered in the law previous to the Code. Its specific mention in canon 1106 has been adjudged in the light of the opinions of present day canonists and moral theologians,[20] as above indicated, to refer to cases wherein scandal is given actively rather than passively received.

Article III. Grave Injury to the Sanctity of Marriage

Complementing the possibility of the revelation of a Marriage of Conscience because of scandal, the law imparts the same power to the local Ordinary when a grave injury to the sanctity of marriage is imminent. Publication of the marriage in this instance would be undertaken essentially to safeguard the sanctity and dignity of the sacrament, and not, as in the cases of scandal, to protect the faithful.[21]

According to the words appearing in the law itself,[22] three elements must coexist in a given case before the local Ordinary may feel himself free to make a Marriage of Conscience public because

18 Genicot-Salsmans, *loc. cit.;* Noldin-Schmitt, *op. cit.* II, n. 105; Vermeersch, *Theologiae Moralis,* II, n. 113.

19 *Supra,* p. 37.

20 Cf. canon 6, 3.

21 Payen, *De Matrimonio,* II, n. 1947.

22 ". . . obligatio . . . non extenditur ad casum quo . . . gràvis erga matrimonii sanctitatem iniuria ex secreti observantia immineat."—Canon 1106.

of an impending injury to the marriage. In the first place, a truly grave injury must be involved, for example, an attempt by one or both of the parties to enter another marriage, to practice adultery, or to cohabit with someone other than the true spouse. Secondly, the existence and the continuation of the injury to the sacrament must be rendered easier precisely because of the observance of secrecy. The threat of harm which finds its origin in the preservation of the secret character of the marriage would best be removed in consequence of the cessation of any further obligation of secrecy. Thirdly, the injury in question cannot be one already completely past; it must be one that is present or at least imminent.[23]

In support of his opinion as here subscribed to, namely, that these three elements are simultaneously postulated in every case if a grave injury to the Sacrament is to become at all allegeable, Payen proposes an interesting case wherein the adultery of one of the parties did not liberate the local Ordinary from his obligation of maintaining secrecy. In the case as it is given, though the injury to the sanctity of marriage was certainly grave, yet the secret character of the marriage did not particularly facilitate the commission of the sins, the culprit had already repented of his sins, and his accomplice had departed never to return, sometime before the local Ordinary considered taking action. Therefore, though at the time of the adultery the local Ordinary might have made use of his faculty granted in canon 1106 to reveal the marriage, in the passage of time the circumstances changed so that it could no longer be certainly stated that the sanctity of the Marriage of Conscience was being injured because of the adultery of one of the parties. The acts of adultery had ceased at the time selected for the divulgation of the Marriage of Conscience, and no injury impended from the continued observance of secrecy, for no injury was present in fact.[24]

[23] Payen, *De Matrimonio,* II, n. 1948.

[24] The actual case is as follows. Matthew entered a Marriage of Conscience with Lucy, which union endured secretly and uneventfully for three years. During the fourth year Matthew frequently committed adultery with Bertha, a married woman, who subsequently left the city with her husband never to return. Lucy knew nothing of the sins, but the injury to the marriage of Bertha was known by quite a few persons.

In the days before any definite legislation appeared on this subject, it had not been unusual for persons who were secretly validly married to decide to marry new spouses, and even in the Church.[25] The *Satis Vobis* did much to eliminate the possible arising of such a situation, and the Code of Canon Law has definitely provided the local Ordinary with adequate means of protecting the sanctity of the marriage contract when parties to a Marriage of Conscience abuse the favor accorded them by partaking in actions injurious to the sacrament.

Article IV. Failure to Have the Children Baptized

Persons living in a Marriage of Conscience are held by at least the same obligation to have their offspring baptized as the members of the faithful living in public marriage. Baptism must follow birth as soon as it is reasonably possible,[26] and those who are responsible for the baptisms are bound by a grave obligation in this regard.[27] Precisely the amount of time which is allowed before the parents become guilty of grave neglect has not been determined in the law. The opinions concerning the duration of the permissible time differ widely. Cappello allows only three or four days.[28] Ayrinhac extends the time to eight or ten days, unless a particular statute prescribes

The pastor and the Bishop also knew of the twofold adultery, since they knew of the Marriage of Conscience. Sometime after the departure of Bertha Matthew repented, and the local Ordinary was desirous of knowing whether he would be able to, and whether he should, divulge the fact of the marriage of Matthew and Lucy. The adultery had taken place and had injured the marriage of Bertha in any event. The circumstance of Matthew being a party to a Marriage of Conscience simply made the adultery and the injury twofold. But, the possible injury to the sanctity of the Marriage of Conscience was a matter of the past. It was no longer existent at the time the local Ordinary became interested in investigating his obligations in the case.—*De Matrimonio,* II, n. 1948, 1949.

[25] Benedictus XIV, ep. encycl. *Satis Vobis,* 17 nov. 1741, § 2—*Fontes,* n. 319.

[26] "Infantes quamprimum baptizentur."—Canon 770.

[27] Canon 770.

[28] *De Sacramentis,* I, n. 149.

otherwise.[29] The opinion most favorable, from the viewpoint of the time allowed, is that of Vermeersch-Creusen who hold that a delay beyond a month without a cause, or two months with a cause, would constitute grave matter.[30] Moral theologians likewise have failed to agree on a commonly accepted time limit for the reception of baptism by infants.[31]

Obviously the meaning of *quamprimum* in canon 770 cannot be determined with absolute exactness. However, if the law desired to specify the exact number of days it could easily have done so, but actually circumstances are so varied in different instances that a general law deciding the time limit would not be desirable.[32] None the less, it is necessary to propose some norm, since the neglect to have children baptized not only brings personal guilt to those living in a Marriage of Conscience, but their culpable carelessness releases the local Ordinary from his obligation of secrecy, so that he may reveal the marriage if he so desires. This last added circumstance regarding the possibility of revealing secret marriage is, of course, not discovered in cases of ordinary neglect.

The amount of time allowed may be specified in a statute of the Bishop.[33] In places where such a law exists the difficulty disappears, since the statute would bind in every case, unless the contrary were so stated. When urgent necessity exists, as in danger of death, the problem likewise is not present, for no delay could be allowed.[34] If one abstracts from cases governed by urgent necessity and particular statute, the opinion of Vermeersch-Creusen seems to be the most acceptable and useful standard to employ in deciding the extent of time allowed before parents may be accused of grave neglect. Therefore, if baptism in a given case has been postponed without a cause

[29] *Legislation on the Sacraments in the New Code of Canon Law*, (New York: Longmans Green & Co., 1928), p. 55.

[30] *Epitome*, II, n. 52.

[31] Genicot-Salsmans, *Institutiones Theologiae Moralis*, II, n. 146; Noldin-Schmitt, *Summa Theologiae Moralis*, III, n. 66; Vermeersch, *Theologiae Moralis*, III, n. 229.

[32] Woywod, *Practical Commentary on the Code*, I, 353.

[33] Vermeersch-Creusen, *Epitome*, II, n. 52; Woywod, *loc. cit.*

[34] Canon 771; Genicot-Salsmans, *Institutiones Theologiae Moralis*, II, n. 146.

beyond a month, the local Ordinary may consider himself free of his obligation to preserve secrecy concerning the fact of the Marriage of Conscience of the parents. It would be well for him to investigate the circumstances in each case, however, since it is quite possible that a cause may exist which has necessitated the delay, in which instance the parties would have two months to fulfill their obligation.

The local Ordinary may consider himself absolved from observing his obligation of secrecy because of neglect to have the children baptized only when the alleged non-baptism concerns the children of the Marriage of Conscience, not of any other marriage.[35] Neglect to have the offspring of another marriage baptized, such as a widow's children by another marriage, or the children of an illegitimate union[36] may not, according to the law, be rectified by means of a revelation of the strictly secret marriage of the parties even though they be guilty. Divulgation might be permitted for other reasons in such a situation, but, consistently with the strict interpretation of these exceptional regulations, one cannot include in the law more than it allows.[37]

The ministers best qualified for the baptism of the children are the local Ordinary who granted permission for the marriage, and the priest who assisted at the ceremony. The reasons for preferring

[35] ". . . parentes non curent filios ex tali matrimonio susceptos baptizari".—Canon 1106.

[36] All types of children who are born and remain illegitimate are here included, since none of these could ever be said to have been born of a Marriage of Conscience. Legitimacy and legitimation require in their concepts that the children be either actually begotten of a valid marriage, or regarded as begotten in a valid marriage by a fiction of the law. Adulterine children, those who were the fruit of sacrilege, and other spurious children cannot be designated at any time as begotten of a valid marriage, or in the case of a Marriage of Conscience *ex tali matrimonio*. Therefore, the failure to have such children baptized would not of itself relax the local Ordinary's obligation to preserve secrecy concerning the fact of a strictly secret marriage. Cf. canons 1114, 1116, 1051; Gasparri, *De Matrimonio,* II, n. 1118; McDevitt, *Legitimacy and Legitimation,* The Catholic University of America Canon Law Studies, n. 138 (Washington, D. C.: The Catholic University of America Press, 1941) pp. 84, 125, 152.

[37] Canon 19.

these persons are to safeguard the secret character of the marriage, to eliminate the necessity of using false names, and to facilitate the administration of the sacrament without the encountering of opposition from a priest who would justifiably desire to know something of the parents of a child presented for baptism. In the event that the priest selected for the baptism is the one who originally witnessed the Marriage of Conscience, though now not the pastor of the parties, the requisite permission for baptizing lawfully should be received from the local Ordinary,[38] who is competent, and who always knows of the marriage.[39]

Article V. Neglect to Inform the Local Ordinary when Baptism Is Given Under Assumed Names

Another circumstance liberating the local Ordinary from his obligation of preserving secrecy regarding a Marriage of Conscience, exists when parents have observed the regulations regarding the baptism of their children, and in so doing have supplied the priest with assumed names for the parents and the children as they are permitted to do, but have neglected to inform the local Ordinary of the facts of the birth and the baptism of the child within thirty days of the

[38] Canon 738, 1.

[39] Hilling observes that in practice difficulties could arise regarding the registration of the baptism of a child born of a Marriage of Conscience if the pastor of the place of baptism knows nothing of the marriage. He maintains that the pastor is obliged to record the name of the child in accord with the prescriptions of canon 777, § 2, which treats of the manner of recording the baptisms of illegitimate children—"Eherechtliche Kontroversen und Probleme,"—*Archiv für katholisches Kirchenrecht* (Vols. I-VI [1857-1861], Innsbruck; Vols. VI— [1862—], Mainz), CV (1925), 108-111. If the pastor has positively no knowledge of the secret marriage this course of action would seem necessary. However, in this situation the real names of the parents and of the child need not be given, unless the parties desire to divulge their marriage at the time of their child's baptism. The true record must be forwarded within thirty days to the local Ordinary, and the obligation of following this manner of proceeding rests with the parties of the marriage.

completion of these acts.[40] The thirty days allowed would best be measured from the time of baptism, according to the apparent meaning of the law.[41]

The text of canon 1106 requires that, when children have been baptized under assumed names, a notice or record of both the birth and the baptism must be forwarded within thirty days. Therefore, the obligation binds from the day of baptism, and not the day of birth. The period of time allowed will normally be computed as a continuous duration since the parents can not plead ignorance of their obligations and hence can not point to any hindrance in respect of its fulfillment during the allotted period.[42] On the other hand, if altogether extraordinary circumstances make it impossible to forward the required report within thirty days, the time allotted will have to be extended until the parents will have had at their disposal thirty days within which they could send the necessary information to the local Ordinary.[43] In computing the time which is allowed to the parents in a given case, before they can be accused of culpable neglect, the day of baptism would not be counted, and the period would end with the completion of the thirtieth day.[44]

This case was comprehended by the old law, which insisted that the offspring of a Marriage of Conscience be baptized in Church as other infants.[45] The same manner of proceeding is to be recommended even today.[46] Again, in the absence of precise directions in the Code of Canon Law regarding the manner of making the report of the birth and baptism, the regulations of the old law should be followed when they do not contradict the new law.[47] Therefore, when the secret nature of the marriage requires that persons have their children baptized without indicating the child's parentage, or

40 Canon 1106.

41 Canon 18.

42 Canon 35.

43 Canon 35.

44 Canon 34, § 3, 3°.

45 Benedictus XIV, ep. encycl. *Satis Vobis,* 17 nov. 1741, § 11—*Fontes,* n. 319.

46 Payen, *De Matrimonio,* II, n. 1942.

47 Canon 6, 2°, 3°.

when parents submit assumed names for entry in the paorchial baptismal register, the father of the child, or in the event of his death the mother, must forward the necessary information to the local Ordinary.[48] This report is to be made personally, or through letters written by those bearing the obligation, or by enlisting the services of a worthy person who can fulfill exactly the required office.[49]

There are to be incorporated in this report indications of the time and place of the baptism, of whether the parentage was simply concealed or expressed under assumed names, and of assurance regarding the legitimacy of the offspring. When this report reaches the local Ordinary the facts included therein shall be entered in the books retained for that purpose in the Secret Archives, which process is to be discussed in a subsequent chapter. The following of the regulations given for Marriages of Conscience regarding the baptism of the children in no way modifies the essential obligations concerning baptism [50] and its registration [51] as asserted in the common law, though certain changes in carrying out the law must be observed. One of the essential purposes of the laws made in favor of strictly secret marriages is to ensure the welfare and to vindicate the legitimacy of the children born of these unions. Therefore records of these facts are demanded. If a child is baptized under the true names of its parents and if this can be accomplished without any sacrificing of the secrecy of the Marriage of Conscience, inasmuch as the minister of baptism is also the priest who assisted at the secret marriage, then a complete report must be sent to the local Ordinary without delay, [52] but not necessarily within thirty days. The power extended to the local Ordinary of revealing a Marriage of Conscience after the lapse of thirty days when he has not been informed of the birth and of the baptism of the offspring may be utilized only when the baptism was conferred either under assumed names on the part of the parents or without the indication of any names whatsoever.

[48] Benedictus XIV, ep. encycl. *Satis Vobis,* 17 nov. 1741, § 11—*Fontes,* n. 319.

[49] *Loc. cit.*

[50] Canon 770.

[51] Canon 771, § 1.

[52] Canon 777, § 1.

Article VI. Neglect of the Christian Education of the Children

In the old law an injunction to educate the children of a Marriage of Conscience in piety and good morals was to be included in the prenuptial admonition.[53] Neglect of the christian education of the children of such a marriage in the Code of Canon Law would furnish the local Ordinary with grounds for exposing the fact of the marriage.[54] Some norms must be proposed, therefore, as criteria by which the competent superior may determine what constitutes religious education, and when its neglect will liberate the local Ordinary from his obligation of keeping secret the fact of the particular Marriage of Conscience.

The Church, from ancient times the unequalled leader and patron of all sincerely interested in true education of soul and body, in modern times, with the rapid and widespread growth of secular education with its many attendant dangers, has not hesitated to emphasize the obligations of parents to imbue their offspring with the principles of their religion, and preserve them from all influences repugnant to the integrity of their faith and morals.[55] By divine and canon law all catholic parents must provide that certain specific phases of the religious education of their children are attended to. The children must be baptized,[56] and receive adequate catechetical instruction.[57] Upon reaching the age of reason, they should receive the Holy Eucharist.[58] Their education should be pursued in Catholic institutions, unless the local Ordinary is of the opinion that secular schools may be attended without the danger of perversion.[59] This obligation of parents to watch sedulously over their children's religious education

[53] Benedictus XIV, ep. encycl. *Satis Vobis,* 17 nov. 1741 § 9—*Fontes,* n. 319.

[54] Canon 1106.

[55] Pius XI, encycl. *Casti connubii,* 31 dec. 1930—*AAS,* XXII (1930), 539.

[56] Canons 770; 747; 748.

[57] Canon 1335.

[58] Canon 860.

[59] Canon 1374.

is a most grave one,[60] and it embraces the whole moral and religious life of the child from birth till it progresses successively through life's various stages to elect its own future as an adult.[61] The hierarchy of the Church in the United States has shown great solicitude over the religious education of children, declaring it to be the foundation of all true civilization and most necessary both in the home and in the school.[62]

Neglect to have the children of a Marriage of Conscience baptized, or to follow the prescribed form of registration when it is demanded, has already been demonstrated to constitute grounds for the local Ordinary to reveal the fact of the marriage. Here demands for christian education are placed beyond baptism with the same release from the obligation of secrecy following in cases of carelessness. All parents who deliberately deliver up their children to non-catholic education automatically incur a punishment,[63] and in Marriages of Conscience not only does this penalty operate, but the local Ordinary is liberated from his obligation of secrecy when neglect of the religious education of the offspring occurs, whether or not positive attempts were made to educate the children under non-Catholic auspices. Upon the local Ordinary's discovery that the parties to a strictly secret marriage are not providing for their childrens' religious instruction and their reception of the sacraments, though they have had them baptized, or that they allow their children to frequent secular schools when no need for it exists, and against the wishes of the Bishop, he should consider himself liberated from the obligation he assumed at the outset of the marriage to maintain secrecy concerning the fact of its celebration.

60 Canon 1113.

61 Cappello, *De Sacramentis,* III, pars II, n. 743, 744; Payen, *De Matrimonio,* II, n. 2146, 2147; Vlaming, *Praelectiones Iuris Matrimonii,* II, n. 667; Wernz-Vidal, *Ius Canonicum,* V, n. 602.

62 *Acta et Decreta Concilii Plenarii Baltimorensis Tertii* (1884), pp. LXXXII, LXXXIII, LXXXV, 153, 213.

63 Canon 2319, § 1, 4°.

CHAPTER IX

REGISTRATION AND SUPERVISION OF THE RECORDS OF THESE MARRIAGES

Canon 1107.—Matrimonium conscientiae non est adnotandum in consueto matrimoniorum ac baptizatorum libro, sed in peculiari libro servando in secreto Curiae archivo de quo in can. 379.

ARTICLE I. MANNER OF INSCRIBING AND PRESERVING THESE RECORDS

SEEKING in every possible way to safeguard the secrecy so intimately connected with all phases of the procedure detailed in the law for Marriages of Conscience, the legislator added another helpful factor in the regulations which define the mode of registering these marriages. The new law does not permit the entering of the records of such marriages in the ordinary marriage and baptismal registers.[1] Special books are to be reserved in the Secret Archives of the Diocesan Curia to receive these records. Deep concern is manifested in the law for documents retained in the Secret Archives, which is evidenced by the fact that detailed directions have been supplied with regard to the erection, contents, use and custody of these Archives.[2]

The depository for secret documents should be so constructed as not to be removable; in other words, it ought to be a vault or safe built into the wall. The door of this chamber should be provided with two different locks to be opened with different keys, of which one should be kept by the Bishop or the Apostolic Administrator, and the other by the Vicar General, or, in his default, by

[1] Cappello, *De Sacramentis,* III, pars II, n. 724; Wernz-Vidal, *Ius Canonicum,* V, n. 570; Petrovits, *The New Church Law on Matrimony,* p. 370; Woywod, *Practical Commentary on the Code,* I, 697.

[2] Canon 379; Louis, *Diocesan Archives,* p. 70.

the Chancellor.[3] The prescriptions regarding the burning of documents retained in the Secret Archives[4] certainly do not pertain to the records of the Marriages of Conscience still unknown, which are inscribed in the books required by law.

It has been stated by Louis that no mention is discovered in the law of the arrangement to be used for the writings in the Secret Archives. The same author suggests that the documents in each instance be placed in a separate folder chronologically, with the names of those involved in the case on the outside. These folders are eventually to be arranged alphabetically with a new classification started after a period of years. Perhaps such an arrangement my well be an excellent one for most documents coming under the surveillance of the custodian of the Secret Archives, but in regard to Marriages of Conscience it would be at variance with the law, and not at all satisfactory. There is an explicit demand for the registration of these marriages and the subsequent baptisms in a book or books.[5] This form of recording Marriages of Conscience is simply commanded in reiteration of the old law, which demanded that the original documents testifying to facts concerning strictly secret marriages be transcribed exactly, and without delay, in books.[6] These books should be similar to the ordinary parish registers, and the book form is more appropriate than folders, since there would be less danger of losing or mislaying the necessary information. Therefore the manner of preserving the records pertaining to Marriages of Conscience in the Secret Archives is not optional, but prescribed by law.

The law in force before the Code of Canon Law required that there be kept two distinct and separate books in which the records of the Marriages of Conscience and the subsequent baptisms, respec-

[3] These are the major provisions of canon 379. A complete and most useful exposition of the requirements of the law in this regard may be found in Louis, *Diocesan Archives*, pp. 70-86.

[4] Canon 379, § 1.

[5] ". . . non est adnotandum in consueto libro . . . sed in peculiari libro servando.—Canon 1107.

[6] Benedictus XIV, ep. encycl. *Satis Vobis*, 17 nov. 1741, § 10, § 11—*Fontes*, n. 319.

tively, could be preserved.[7] Modern authors have chosen simply to repeat the words of the present legislation, which, on first reading, would seem to demand but one book in which the records of both the marriages and the baptisms would be kept.[8] The law itself states that these records be preserved, not in the customary book of marriages and baptisms, but in a special book.[9] However, marriages and baptisms customarily are recorded in separate books, at least this is the obvious meaning of the law on this point,[10] and the common practice. Therefore, the logical conclusion from a careful reading of the law is that separate books should be maintained in the Secret Archives to record the Marriages of Conscience and the subsequent baptisms. This arrangement if preferable because it is in agreement with the previous legislation on the subject, which should not be deserted in cases of doubt as to whether a discrepancy exists between the old and the new law.[11]

No explicit statement in the present law declares what the authority of these books might be. In recurring to the old law one finds that these books were to possess the same authority as the ordinary parochial marriage and baptismal registers.[12] An equal degree of authority is likewise conferred on them in the present day.[13]

The exact method to be followed in the entering of the records under discussion has not been designated. Formerly a complete record of the marriage was to be forwarded to the local Ordinary, without

[7] Benedict XIV, detailing the manner in which the documents were to be recorded, directed that they be transcribed in a book, "prorsus distincto ab altero, in quo Matrimonia publice contracta de more adnotantur". In the next paragraph he required a separate book for the registering of baptisms. "Liber, in quem Baptizatorum, ac utriusque Parentes nomina referentur, distingui debeat ab altero Matrimoniorum".—*Ibid.*, § 10, § 11—*Fontes*, n. 319.

[8] Cappello, *De Sacramentis*, III, pars II, n. 724; Wernz-Vidal, *Ius Canonicum*, V, n. 570; Payen, *De Matrimonio*, II, n. 1942; Petrovits, *The New Church Law on Matrimony*, p. 370.

[9] Canon 1107.

[10] Canons 470, § 1, § 3; 777, § 1; 1103, § 1.

[11] Canon 6, § 4.

[12] Benedictus XIV, ep. encycl. *Satis Vobis*, 17 nov. 1741, § 14—*Fontes*, n. 319.

[13] Payen, *De Matrimonio*, II, n. 1942.

delay, after the ceremony, and the records of baptism also were to be sent within the required time. A trustworthy person appointed by the Bishop was to make the entries in the special books as soon as they were received, and the actual original records were to be preserved in an even more hidden place by the Bishop himself.[14]

These regulations are still operative for the greater part, since records at least as complete as the ordinary parochial records of marriage and baptism must be sent to the local Ordinary by the priest assisting at these ceremonies, that they may be recorded in the special book. Of course if the local Ordinary assists at the Marriage of Conscience or administers baptism to a child of a marriage of this kind he could simply enter the records in the proper books himself, without writing out any other records. The custody and use of the Diocesan Secret Archives is quite definitely restricted to the Bishop, or to persons acting lawfully in his place, or with his permission.[15] But precisely what persons may inscribe new records is not determined. The inventory periodically prescribed[16] most probably may be made by the Chancellor provided that he has taken an oath of secrecy.[17]

In resorting to the law itself one finds that canon 379, § 1, demands that the writings in the Secret Archives be guarded most cautiously, and, even when they must be destroyed in accord with the law, a summary of their contents must be kept. The footnote to this canon in the Gasparri edition of the Code contains a reference to the *Satis Vobis,* § 10, § 11, § 14. These sections of the encyclical define how Marriages of Conscience are to be recorded, and who is to perform the task. Consequent to this interpretation given by Cardinal Gasparri, as deduced from the old law, it seems correct to say that the Bishop may appoint a trustworthy priest to record the Marriages of Conscience if he does not desire to do it himself. Naturally the priest thus commissioned would need the additional

[14] Benedict XIV, ep. encycl. *Satis Vobis,* 17 nov. 1741, § 10, § 11, § 14—*Fontes,* n. 319.

[15] Canons 379, § 3, § 4; 380; 381; Coronata, *Institutiones Iuris Canonici,* I, n. 429; Louis, *Diocesan Archives,* pp. 75-80, 83.

[16] Canon 379, § 2.

[17] Coronata, *loc. cit.;* Louis, *op. cit.,* p. 75.

permission of the Bishop Ordinary to open the Secret Archives.[18] A judicious choice here also would be the Chancellor, who is the ordinary legal custodian of the archives which are not secret.[19] However, the priest selected would, in every case, be bound by the same secrecy that binds all who know of the strictly secret marriage before its divulgation.

The notations in the secret books must be complete, indicating in addition to the usual facts whether the promises to keep the laws regarding the avoidance of scandal, the elimination of injury to the sacrament, the procuring of the baptism and the christian education of the children were made by the parties, and whether the promise of secrecy was given by all concerned. These facts could be noted in the same manner in which the mention of the fact of a granted dispensation is included in the ordinary marriage registers. If the local Ordinary desired to preserve, in addition to the records which constitute the primary legal proof, all the documents received in each case, he may keep these in a separate file in the Secret Archives.

Formerly personal supervision of the actual original documents, even after the registration, was necessary, since there were no specific regulations regarding Secret Archives.[20] At the present time however, the enactments of the Code of Canon Law have made the Diocesan Secret Archives the most secret depository in the Diocese wherein confidential information may be kept.[21] There is no obligation and little advantage, then, in preserving the original documents at all at the present time, since they would also be kept in the Secret Archives with the books in which the pertinent facts have been entered. Such a method would simply multiply records and lead to the confusion attendant upon keeping double and identical records of the same facts in the same place. The local Ordinary may, and would wisely, destroy the original documents once he is certain that the facts contained therein have been accurately and fully recorded.

In the recording of public marriages notices of the fact of mar-

18 Coronata, *Institutiones Iuris Canonici,* I, n. 429; Louis, *Diocesan Archives,* p. 83.

19 Canon 372, § 1.

20 Louis, *Diocesan Archives,* p. 20.

21 Louis, *op. cit.,* p. 70.

riage in each case are to be entered in the baptismal books where the baptisms of the parties were originally recorded.[22] Such notations are not to be made nor are notices to be sent when the marriage is a Marriage of Conscience. Acting in this way would endanger the essential secrecy of the marriage.[23] If, in the course of time, a Marriage of Conscience is divulged it should be recorded in the ordinary marriage register and in the proper baptismal registers at the command of the local Ordinary,[24] and if there are records of baptisms they should also be transferred. This course of action is to be pursued whether the divulgation proceeds from the decision of the local Ordinary or of the parties, and even when the fact of secret marriage has become public from the culpable imprudence of others.[25] For the transcription of the record of a Marriage of Conscience into the parochial marriage register, Wernz-Vidal helpfully recommend that it be placed after the last recorded marriage, but with a notation in the place in the book in which it would have appeared if the marriage had not been celebrated secretly.[26] This suggestion could also be followed out in the transferring to other books or registers the individual records of specific baptisms.

ARTICLE II. WHO MAY ISSUE AND WHO MAY DEMAND COPIES OF THESE RECORDS

When it is necessary to inscribe new records in the special books in the Secret Archives they may be opened and the additional information written down in the proper places.[27] If a petition is presented for a copy of a record in these books the local Ordinary as custodian of the Secret Archives [28] and the ultimately responsible authority in matters concerning Marriage of Conscience, or his law-

[22] Canon 1103, § 2; S. C. de Sacr., instr., 29 iun. 1941, n. 11, d, e—*AAS,* XXXIII (1941), 306; *The Jurist,* II (1942), Supplement, p. 8.

[23] Canon 470, § 2; Wernz-Vidal, *Ius Canonicum,* V, n. 570.

[24] Cappello, *De Sacramentis,* III, par II, n. 724; Wernz-Vidal, *loc. cit.*

[25] Cappello, *loc. cit.*

[26] *Loc. cit.*

[27] Cappello, *De Sacramentis,* III, pars II, n. 724; Wernz-Vidal, *Ius Canonicum,* V, n. 570.

[28] Canon 379, § 3.

ful successors in this trust,[29] should decide whether the desired copy of the record ought to be issued.

The instances in which copies of these records may be demanded is extremely limited. Only those who find it necessary to prove that they took part in the ceremony have the right to seek authentic copies of the records, and then only when proof of this fact is not otherwise obtainable.[30] Such a request must also be prompted by the serious need of these records for the administration of justice, or to safeguard the parties.[31] A justifiable demand would be that of one of the parties who must submit a true marriage record that ecclesiastical judges may be able to determine their competence. A request founded in requirements of the civil law would not merit action by the Bishop. The civil authorities possess no right to require that the Bishop Ordinary reveal information contained in books in the Secret Archives, or that he hand over authentic transcriptions from them.[32]

When marriage or baptismal records are necessary in accord with the demands of the law for the further reception of the Sacraments on the part of the children of Marriages of Conscience,[33] the local Ordinary in whose possession the records in question remain must decide on the manner of supplying the needed information. If the necessity has endured of keeping the Marriage of Conscience and consequent baptisms in question secret, he may allow the use of a record which employs the use of assumed names if the record was originally inscribed in that manner in the parish register. He might, again, suggest to the parties desirous of obtaining a record that they

[29] Canon 1104.

[30] Cappello, *De Sacramentis,* III, pars II, n. 724.

[31] Benedictus XIV, ep. encycl. *Satis Vobis,* 17 nov. 1741, § 10—*Fontes,* n. 319; Wernz-Vidal, *loc. cit.*

[32] S. C. C., *pro Italia superiore datum,* a. 1851—*Coll. Lac.,* VI, 275. This prescription still obtains in the present law.—Wernz-Vidal, *loc. cit.*

[33] Authentic records or testimonials concerning the reception of baptism are required to fulfill the demands placed in canons 786, 968, 1021; likewise a marriage record must be submitted as proof of legitimacy by those seeking sacred orders, cf. canon 984, 1°.

secure sworn statements in proof of the facts in question, or if the further reception of the Sacraments is to take place in his own jurisdiction he could administer these Sacraments himself and thereby obviate all difficulties, since he possesses the required proof in his own Secret Archives, and his personal use of it would in no way endanger the continuance of secrecy.

CHAPTER X

RELATED INCIDENTAL QUESTIONS

ARTICLE I. THE MARRIAGE OF CONSCIENCE IN ORIENTAL CANON LAW

NOT only has the universal authority of the Church determined the norms necessary to be followed by Latin Catholics in contracting Marriages of Conscience, but sufficient attention has been given to the approval of regulations which are to be followed by Oriental Catholics who desire to enter a strictly secret marriage. The law binding Orientals in the external forum in this regard is not founded in the prescriptions of the *Satis Vobis,*[1] but has been developed from custom and diocesan law.

Permission among Orientals, with the exception of the Italo-Greeks, is to be sought from the proper Patriarch or Bishop. It is interesting to note that Vicars of these competent persons may also grant permission, and that no mention of the need of a special mandate is made. Urgent causes are to be proposed as reasons for the seeking of the permission, and once the marriage has been contracted it is not to be inscribed in the common book of marriages, but in a special book which is to be preserved under the custody and seal of the Bishop.[2] Petitions of Oriental Catholics to contract Marriages of Conscience in the internal forum, non-sacramental or sacramental, will be forwarded to the Sacred Tribunal of the Penitentiary in the same manner that Latin Catholics present their requests to that competent Tribunal.[3]

1 Benedictus XIV, ep. encycl. 17 nov. 1741—*Fontes,* n. 319.

2 This method is described in Cappello, *De Sacramentis* III, pars II, n. 928.

3 S. C. pro Eccl. Orient., resp., 26 iul. 1930—*AAS,* XXII (1930), 394; Bouscaren, *Canon Law Digest,* I, 174.

Article II. Relation of the Powers of the Sacred Penitentiary to Those of the Local Ordinary

It has already been stated that the faculty granted by the common law to the local Ordinary to permit Marriages of Conscience in the external forum finds its counterpart in the same power possessed by the Sacred Penitentiary to allow these strictly secret marriages in the forum of conscience, sacramental or extra-sacramental.[4] No conflict exists, therefore, since the powers of these respective authorities operate in distinct forums. As a consequence, if a petition to enter a Marriage of Conscience has been denied by the proper local Ordinary of the parties, they may present their request to the Sacred Penitentiary without any mention of the previous refusal.[5]

The competence of this Tribunal has recently been again emphasized as comprehending all cases in which the faithful desire relief from occult spiritual ills.[6] It is competent to grant favors denied by other authorities because, while the refusal is sometimes necessary for the public welfare, the private good of the individual, with which the Sacred Penitentiary is principally concerned, always prevails.[7]

Of some practical application here is the case in which a request to enter a Marriage of Conscience denied by the Sacred Penitentiary is presented, after refusal, to the petitioners' proper local Ordinary. Some authors claim that a favor denied by the Sacred Penitentiary can be validly granted by the respective local Ordinary in the external forum without his obtaining assent from the Sacred Penitentiary. They base their claim on the fact that the words of canon 43 [8]

[4] *Supra*, p. 65.

[5] There is not found in the law any restriction which limits this manner or method. Cf. canons 43, 44.

[6] Pius XI, const. *Quae divinitus*, 25 mart. 1935—*AAS*, XXVII (1935), 79; *Apollinaris*, VIII (1935), 181.

[7] Kubelbeck, *The Sacred Penitentiaria and its Relations to Faculties of Ordinaries and Priests*, p. 42.

[8] "Gratia ab una Sacra Congregatione vel Officio Romanae Curiae denegata, invalide ab alia Sacra Congregatione vel Officio aut a loci Ordinario, etsi potestatem habente, conceditur sine assensu Sacrae Congregationis vel Officii quocum vel quibuscum agi coeptum fuit . . .".

refer only to a denial by a Congregation or an Office, whereas the Sacred Penitentiary is a Tribunal.[9]

This claim is denied by most of the canonists who refer to the question,[10] and rightly so, for, as Cicognani indicates,[11] if a favor were denied by the Sacred Penitentiary, but were later granted by another agency in the external forum, the original internal forum denial would no longer be effectual. The reason for this is found in the fact that what is valid for the external forum is valid for the internal forum, but not vice versa. This ought not to be, nor is there adequate reason for supporting such a seeming contradiction. In the light of the whole of canon 43 the argument declaring that the Penitentiary is not included in the terms Congregation or Office because it is a Tribunal falls. The final clause, *"salvo iure S. Poenitentiaria pro foro interno"* indicates that the terms Congregation and Office are not to be understood in this canon as excluding all Tribunals, but rather as embracing the Sacred Penitentiary, which grants for the internal forum the favors granted by the Congregations and Offices for the external forum. Under any other interpretation the insertion of the clause just mentioned becomes useless and meaningless.[12] The correct conclusion is: when a petition to enter a Marriage of Conscience has been refused by the Tribunal of the Sacred Penitentiary, then permission can not validly be given by the local Ordinary without the assent of the Penitentiary.

In a given occult case, persons who are desirous of obtaining from the Sacred Penitentiary the permission to enter a Marriage of Conscience may address their petition directly to that Tribunal if they

[9] Cappello, *Summa,* I, n. 145; Michiels, *Normae Generales Iuris Canonici,* (2 vols., Lublin, Polonia: Universitas Catholica, 1929), II, 181, 182.

[10] Chelodi, *Ius de Personis,* p. 138, note 3; Coronata, *Institutiones Iuris Canonici,* I, n. 63; Maroto, *Institutiones,* I, 322; Vermeersch-Creusen, *Epitome,* I, n. 156; Ayrinhac, *General Legislation in the New Code of Canon Law* (New York: Longmans, Green & Co., 1925), p. 150; Cicognani, *Canon Law,* p. 721; O'Neill, *Papal Rescripts of Favor,* The Catholic University of America Canon Law Studies, n. 57 (Washington, D. C.: The Catholic University of America, 1930), pp. 142, 143.

[11] *Loc. cit.*

[12] O'Neill, *Papal Rescripts of Favor,* p. 143.

so desire.[13] Ordinarily the most convenient arrangement is to enlist the services of one's confessor, pastor, or other priest, and to forward the request in the internal non-sacramental forum.[14] In any event, the names of the petitioners are not to be used, but fictitious names are to be placed in the letter describing the case. This letter is to be forwarded sealed, through the public mails, to the Sacred Penitentiary. In no case is an open letter to be sent to a procurator or agent who will present the letter himself.[15] However, a sealed letter submitted by a procurator would be acceptable. The letter itself may be written in any language. No tax is demanded, and therefore a tax should not be sent. Naturally the correct names and addresses of the persons to whom the response is to be directed should be supplied at the end of the letter, or at least adequate directions as to how the answer may reach its proper destination.[16]

If the requested permission is obtained, the priest consulted in the case must follow strictly the instructions in the rescript and, granted that the rescript was executed in the internal non-sacramental forum, the information contained therein and the resulting marriage, if a Marriage of Conscience is allowed, must be recorded in the book which is kept in the Secret Archives.[17] Cappello says that the actual decree which allowed the marriage must be preserved in the proper parochial archives,[18] but he offers no particular reason for his statement. It would appear to reflect a more uniform and safe method if all the records of these marriages were preserved in the Secret Archives, whether they pertain to the external forum[19] or the internal forum. In fact, once the Marriage of Conscience has

[13] Pius XI, const. *Quae divinitus,* 25 mart. 1925 — *AAS,* XXVII (1935), 79; *Apollinaris,* VIII (1935), 181. (The present manner of addressing mail to the Sacred Penitentiary is: All' Emin. Cardinale Penitenziere Maggiore, Palazzo S. Ufficio, Roma.)

[14] Cappello, *De Sacramentis,* III, pars II, n. 280; Wernz, *Ius Decretalium,* IV, n. 639.

[15] S. Poenit. Ap., monitum (not dated)—*AAS,* XXVII (1935), 62.

[16] Cappello, *De Sacramentis,* III, pars II, n. 288, 290; Coronata, *Compendium Iuris Canonici,* I, n. 626; Vermeersch-Creusen, *Epitome,* I, 375.

[17] Canon 1047.

[18] *De Sacramentis,* III, pars II, n. 289.

[19] *Supra,* p. 127.

been accurately registered in the Secret Archives, there is no obligation to preserve the original document at all, nor would it constitute a valid proof of the celebration of the marriage.

Article III. Divergent Prescriptions of Ecclesiastical and Civil Authorities

The Catholic Church of today, consistently fulfilling the positive command of Her Divine Founder, has brought to the feet of Christ souls from all parts of the world. The political organization of world civil powers includes many member nations who rule the people living in their territories by multiple and variant laws. It is not surprising, therefore, to observe many instances in which the always uniform general law of the Church is at variance with the civil legislations of the several countries. Some few nations have given recognition to God's laws and precepts while on the other hand some prescind completely even from his very existence. It is our good fortune to find ourselves living in a land where freedom of worship is advocated. The maintenance of such a principle presupposes at the very least the existence of a God to worship. Exact observance of civil requirements should and must be practiced whenever it is possible. But in the hierarchy of authorities the prescriptions of Christ and of His Church enjoy a relative precedence over the legislative requirements of all other powers, and primary attention must be paid to ecclesiastical enactments.

Marriages of Conscience celebrated in accord with ecclesiastical regulations find civil recognition in only four countries. Lithuania, Italy and Austria give recognition to these marriages in consequence of the concordats they have completed with the Holy See. The concordat in each case includes an agreement to recognize the civil effects of the Sacrament of matrimony as administered according to the regulations of Canon Law.[20] Spanish law simply allows strictly

[20] The agreement between the Holy See and Lithuania reads as follows: Article XV, "Les marriages célébrés en conformité des prescriptions du code Canonique obtiennent par la même les effets civils". Between the Holy See and Italy: Article XXXIV, "Lo Stato italiano, volendo ridonare all' istituto del matrimonio, che è base della famiglia, dignità conforme alle tradizioni cattoliche del suo popolo, riconosce al

secret marriages to be celebrated in accord with the law of the Church and does not demand any manner of additional civil formalities.[21] However, in this Spanish legisaltion such marriages do not automatically produce their civil effects until, having been published, they are entered in the municipal marriage registers. None the less, these Marriages of Conscience have effect even in civil law in Spain if both parties of the marriage sought a copy of the marriage record entered in the Diocesan Secret Archives from the local Ordinary, and forwarded it to the General Director of the Civil Registers. This person includes in his department a special register in which secret marriages are recorded until they are divulged, in which event the record is transcribed into the ordinary municipal marriage registers.[22]

An interesting case may be mentioned which occurred in Spain, but which because of its circumstances, fell outside the scope of even the favorable laws of that country regarding secret marriages. Two catholics entered marriage civilly, but some time later they separated and the man desired to marry another woman according to the laws of the Church. Canonically the civil marriage was proved invalid because of the failure to observe the substantially required form.[23] Spanish law, however, recognizes such a public civil marriage as valid, as long as both parties stated at the time of the marriage that they no longer embraced the Catholic faith, which certainly had been a circumstance of the case in its origin. The parties had denied their faith that they might not be refused marriage by the civil authorities. On the other hand, the law of Spain does not allow divorce, and it enacts punishments for parties, priests, and judges who permit or favor marriages of previously married persons. Parties

sacramento del matrimonio, disciplinato dal diritto canonico, gli effetti civili". Between the Holy See and Austria; "Die Republik Oesterreich erkennt den gemäss dem kanonischen Recht geschlossenen Ehen die bürgerlichen Rechtswirkungen zu." — Perugini, *Concordata Vigentia Notis Historicis et Iuridicis Declarata,* (Romae: apud custodiam librariam Pont. Instituti utriusque iuris S. Apollinare, 1934), pp. 65, 134, 277.

[21] Cappello, *De Sacramentis,* III, pars II, n. 725; Wernz-Vidal, *Ius Canonicum,* V, n. 570.

[22] Wernz-Vidal, *loc. cit.*

[23] Canon 1099, § 1.

to these marriages are reputed as bigamists. A solution for the problem was found in that the man was allowed to contract an ecclesiastical Marriage of Conscience,[24] with the woman he desired, after a declaration of the nullity of his first marriage had been issued. However, though nothing has been stated regarding the civil recognition of this second marriage, it could hardly be regarded as valid by the State in spite of its recognition of the Marriages of Conscience, since such a stand would involve a contradiction in this instance.

Unfortunately most civil codes completely ignore the possibility of a justifiable desire for the contraction of a strictly secret marriage.[25] Moreover, in many places civil requirements and impediments have been established which find no place in Church legislation. Persons who require marriage to remedy the condition of their souls may find the solution to their difficulties under the law of God, but not under the law of man.[26] However, the situation in such cases is not

[24] *Apollinaris,* IV (1931), 607.

[25] Cappello, *De Sacramentis,* III, pars II, n. 725; Wernz-Vidal, *loc. cit.*

[26] A comparative study of ecclesiastical and civil marriage legislations as they exist in the United States may be found in Alford, *Jus Matrimoniale Comparatum.* A brief summary of the principal points of difference as outlined in the work just mentioned is here proposed.

In twenty-four States and possessions of the United States there are higher age requirements for both men and women than in Canon Law. In five others the age demanded for women is higher, but not for men, and in two others the age for men, but not for women, is higher than the Church requires.—pp. 58-61. In most States the impediment of age renders a marriage voidable.—p. 58. In other words marriage entered with this impediment present would not be rendered null, but subject to a declaration of nullity before the death of the other party unless the contract is even implicitly ratified after the age is attained, v.g. by cohabitation.—pp. 47-55.

There are thirty States wherein marriages are forbidden between white persons and persons of Negro, Indian, or Asiatic origin.—p. 142. In some places likewise Negroes may not marry Indians.—p. 144. Generally this impediment is a diriment one of the first class which consequently renders marriages between these persons civilly void.—p. 144.

Epileptics are forbidden to marry in seventeen States, and those laboring under venereal diseases in twenty-two States, Tuberculosis constitutes a personal impediment in four States, and any contagious disease in four

always simply a hopeless one, even from the viewpoint of civil law. Practically, the civil law would not often present an insurmountable barrier to the contraction of a Marriage of Conscience when not all its precepts could be fulfilled.

In the situation where persons already living together and reputed as validly married desire to contract a Marriage of Conscience, they would often have already been married civilly, or have been living together in circumstances which constitute common law marriage.[27] Therefore they would have fulfilled the prescriptions of the civil law, and the ecclesiastical blessing of their union in the contracting

others.—p. 148. Lepers may not obtain a marriage license in the Canal Zone without a certificate from the public health officer.—p. 150. Disease constitutes a diriment civil impediment in eight States and one Territory.—pp. 149, 151-154.

Poverty is a diriment to civil marriage in one State, and an impeding one in six others.—p. 156.

Marriage in ten States is forbidden to the defendant in a suit for divorce on the grounds of adultery successfully prosecuted by the Plaintiff. —p. 163. Subsequent marriages entered in the State where the divorce was granted would usually be null for the guilty defendant.—p. 164.

All States and Territories require that a civil license be obtained before marriage. However, only seven States and one Territory demand a license for the validity of the marriage.—pp. 200-201.

The canonical notion of dispensation is not known in American Civil Law, though some relaxation in certain cases is permitted, for instance when the woman desiring marriage is already pregnant the law requiring an interval of time between the petition for a license and its concession, or between the issuing of the license and the celebration of the marriage, may be relaxed in thirteen States and one possession. Sixteen other States make some exceptions in cases where the impediment of age is involved.—p. 176. Civil jurists grant that it may be at times arduous to observe the enactments of the law, but they count this as an inevitable consequence of all law since, in every case without exception, the common good is to be preferred. Thus they logically reject at the outset of their reasoning all idea of dispensation.—p. 177.

[27] Common law marriages are recognized as valid in twenty-two States, and the District of Columbia. Persons who contracted such a marriage in a place where it was allowed, may also later live in other States where common law marriages are not permitted, with no danger of the original validity of the marriage being attacked.—Alford, *op. cit.*, pp. 294-295.

of a Marriage of Conscience need in no way become known or be affected by the laws and authorities of the State. This same method may be followed when re-marriage licenses are to be secured by persons who marry the same person twice in the eyes of the civil authorities. The requirement for such licenses has recently been introduced in some places as a precautionary measure. In cases wherein no divorce has intervened, but persons desire only that their marriage be convalidated ecclesiastically by means of the contraction of a Marriage of Conscience, such convalidation, as a blessing of the marriage already civilly existent, would not be remarriage. Civil authorities who do not admit that the marriage bond can be broken save by civil divorce, could hardly in a given case, require a new license for the same parties who go through another ceremony without divorce intervening. If the first civil ceremony was valid civilly and has never been civilly broken, the second ceremony cannot logically be called a civil marriage, or require a civil license.

When a desire to enter a Marriage of Conscience represents the first proposal or attempt of both parties for marriage, and ecclesiastical authorities judge that the permission may be granted, there still remain the civil obligations of applying for and securing a license and, in some places, of passing a physical test. The observance of these prescriptions of civil authorities may at times lead to a violation of the secrecy so necessary in Marriages of Conscience. Many civil codes require that the names of applicants for marriage licenses be printed in the local newspapers. More than that, all who know of the marriage, even if it were not published, that is, the clerks issuing the documents, or also the doctors and nurses in the event that physical tests must be taken, could not feasibly be bound to the secrecy required of all who know of a Marriage of Conscience in the proper sense. The only solution in these instances seems to be that which will allow the Marriages of Conscience, and calls for the fulfillment of the civil requirements only later when the marriage is revealed.

The contraction of marriage may at times be impossible merely because of civil impediments. The simplest solution in such circumstances is that the parties who are so prevented go to a place where the law does not bind so strictly in their case. None the less, it must always be kept in mind that there are times when marriage is most necessary, and is allowed in the eyes of the Church, but not by the State. When the spiritual good of the parties is at stake, permission to contract a Marriage of Conscience, whether it would be recognized civilly or not, would be justifiably granted. To take away from man the natural and primeval right of marriage, to circumscribe in any may the principal ends of marriage laid down in the beginning by God Himself, is beyond the power of any human law.[28]

When health requirements are unnecessarily exacting the words of the saintly Pius XI, condemning those who put the aims of eugenics before the aims of a higher order, should be remembered. He emphatically denounces all who wish, by public authority, to prevent from marrying all who, though naturally fit for marriage, according to certain norms and conjectures of these persons' investigations, would bring forth defective offspring.[29] This opinion was uttered specifically against the proponents of eugenic sterilization, but the principle enunciated remains the same in other cases, for example, when impediments of miscegenation, or racial difference exist. All unprejudiced writers on the subject conclude that the reasons for the existence of these civil impediments are not based on even physiological, or scientific claims, but are founded on the prejudice of the persons living in localities where the impediments exist, and their attempts to maintain the supremacy of the Caucasian race.[30] Children of marriages between Caucasion and Negroes, Asiatics, or Indians, they consider as socially defective. The conjectured possibility of social deficiency in children, if any, is not sufficient reason to deprive man of a natural right.

The ultimate authority to pass judgment on the necessity and advisability of a Marriage of Conscience is the local Ordinary. If, in his prudent discretion, he allows one to take place, his essential obligation in conscience is fulfilled in following the regulations of the Church for these marriages. Civil requirements should certainly be observed precisely when that is at all possible, but they merit only

[28] Leo XIII, encycl. *Rerum novarum,* 15 maii 1891, § 9—*Fontes,* n. 611; *ASS,* XXIII (1890-1891), 641.

[29] Encycl., *Casti connubii,* 31 dec. 1930—*AAS,* XXII (1930), 564.

[30] Alford, *Ius Matrimoniale Comparatum,* p. 143.

secondary consideration when their observance would nullify the ecclesiastical powers of the local Ordinary in his right to allow Marriages of Conscience.

Article IV. Practical Suggestions

Mindful at all times of the necessity of holding intact the completely secret nature of Marriages of Conscience, the local Ordinary would do well to grant the permission for them with the advice that they be celebrated elsewhere than in church, unless precautions have been taken to guarantee that none but those involved will know of the marriage.[31] Ordinarily marriages between catholics should take place in the parochial church,[32] except when the local Ordinary decides to dispense from this requirement in an extraordinary case and for a just and reasonable cause.[33]

Both of these requirements are certainly present when the marriage is to be a Marriage of Conscience. Its whole character is extraordinary and the causes alleged must be most grave and most urgent. These factors constitute sufficient reason, therefore, to permit the strictly secret marriage to take place in a private home. Often, however, the contraction of marriage at home would be attended with no more, or perhaps even less, secrecy than a celebration of it in church. The places most suitable are simply the places where secrecy can best be obtained, for example, the Chancery Office itself, the rectory of the parish where the parties live, or a Catholic hospital.

Before exacting the promises the local Ordinary, or the priest designated to assist at the marriage, should explain their nature and indicate the extent of the implied obligations to those who are to furnish them. All but the parties themselves receive the same promise to secrecy.[34] The promise demanded from the parties should likewise

[31] Marriages of Conscience should take place, "in loco secreto".—Wernz-Vidal, *Ius Canonicum,* V, n. 565.

[32] Canon 1109, § 1.

[33] Canon 1109, § 2.

[34] No definite form has been proposed for these promises. A simple formula would suffice, as: "I, the undersigned, residing at . . . promise to keep as an inviolable secret all knowledge I have of the Marriage of Conscience to be contracted by N. . . . and N. . . . , on the . . .

be prefaced with an instruction regarding its character,[35] and an admonition should be given concerning the necessity of observing the specific demands contained in the law regarding Marriages of Conscience.[36]

day of . . . 19 . I further promise never to reveal in any manner, by word, action, or otherwise, the fact of my having participated as a witness in this strictly secret marriage, or the fact of its having taken place. In the event that circumstances arise which indicate that a revelation of this marriage seems advisable, I shall consult the Bishop of this Diocese, or the priest before whom I am making this promise, and carefully follow his advice, before betraying my knowledge of this Marriage of Conscience in any manner". Each witness shall make the promise, and when the promise has been drawn up in writing it should be signed by the person promising and by the authorized person administering the promise, with the date and place of its execution added in each case.

[35] Because the parties are immediately and continually affected by their promise, and because they may bring it to termination by mutual consent, a somewhat different formula may be used, for example: "I, the undersigned, residing at . . . , having received the permission of the Most Rev. . . . , Bishop of the Diocese of . . . (The Vicar General's name would be inserted here in place of that of the Bishop Ordinary if the Vicar General granted permission in virtue of a special mandate), to enter a Marriage of Conscience with . . . , residing at . . . , promise to observe strict secrecy regarding the fact of my marriage. I promise that I shall in no way divulge its having taken place, unless my spouse and I mutually agree on the matter of its permissible revelation. If such an agreement is reached I shall notify the Bishop of this Diocese, or the priest before whom this marriage is to be entered, of our decision, before or at the time chosen for divulgation".

[36] If the local Ordinary so desires he can ask that the parties of the marriage sign a statement, somewhat in the nature of the *cautiones,* to the effect that they know and understand the obligations incumbent upon them as detailed in canon 1106. The implications of this canon must be correctly understood if they are to be observed not only in good faith but also with an objectively certain conscience.

CONCLUSIONS

1. Gratian, reiterating and summarizing the opinions of his predecessors, denounced clandestine marriages as seriously sinful, yet he supported their validity in cases wherein it could be proved that they were founded on true consent.

2. The authentic legislation in the Decretals of Gregory IX demanded proof for secret marriages, and exhibited the manner of securing it. These marriages were most severely prohibited, and punishments were enunciated for those involved in them; however, they were not declared invalid.

3. The decree *Tametsi* eliminated the possibility of contracting a valid strictly secret marriage in the external forum, but failed to supply adequate substitute legislation to be used in instances wherein secret marriage was most necessary. This lack began to be supplied in the internal forum by the Sacred Penitentiary, which Tribunal allowed, for the first time, true Marriages of Conscience, which were valid and licit as long as the periodically changing and developing prescriptions given for these marriages were followed.

4. In the encyclical letter of Benedict XIV in 1741, Ordinaries were given the power to permit Marriages of Conscience in the external forum, provided that a *causa gravis, urgens et urgentissima,* was present. The records of these marriages and subsequent baptisms of the children of these marriages were to be preserved in special books and closely guarded by the Bishop. Those who failed to observe the special regulations regarding the baptism and recording of the baptisms of children were liable to punishment by the Bishop.

5. At the present time those competent to allow Marriages of Conscience in each jurisdiction are the local Ordinary himself, and the Vicar General exercising ordinary power in virtue of a special mandate. The cause alleged must be verified as most grave and most urgent before permission can validly be given, and it must be certain that the parties are free to enter marriage before the ceremony takes place.

6. The promise given by all who are to know of a marriage of this type is to hold their knowledge as a committed secret. All instruction on the nature of the promises should be given before they are made, and they should be executed in writing and accepted before the ceremony.

7. The obligation of the promise of secrecy made by the local Ordinary is not referable to the cases listed exhaustively in canon 1106.

8. Marriages of Conscience, and baptisms of the offspring of such marriages, are to be recorded exclusively in separate books preserved in the Diocesan Secret Archives. The local Ordinary is the deciding authority in determining whether a record of such marriages may be issued.

9. The Sacred Penitentiary may always be petitioned for permission to enter a Marriage of Conscience in the internal forum, even when the permission has been previously refused in the external forum.

10. In the event of a conflict arising between civil and ecclesiastical authorities regarding the right of baptized persons to marry, a Marriage of Conscience may be allowed if the competent authority thinks that the permission can be justifiably granted.

BIBLIOGRAPHY

SOURCES

Acta Apostolicae Sedis, Commentarium Officiale, Romae, 1909—

Acta et Decreta Concilii Plenarii Baltimorensis Tertii, A.D. MDCCCLXXXIV, Baltimorae: John Murphy, 1886.

Acta et Decreta Sacrorum Conciliorum Recentiorum, Collectio Lacensis 7 vols., Friburgi Brisgoviae, 1870-1890.

Acta Sanctae Sedis, 41 vols., Romae, 1865-1908.

Bouscaren, T. Lincoln, *Canon Law Digest,* 2 vols., Milwaukee: The Bruce Publishing Co., 1934-1943.

Bullarii Romani Continuatio Summorum Pontificum, 19 vols., Prato, 1756-1883.

Bullarium SSmi Domini Nostri Benedicti Papae XIV, 4. ed., 4 vols., Venetiis, 1778.

Canones et Decreta Sacrosancti Oecumenici Concilii Tridentini sub Paulo III, Iulio III, et Pio IV Pontificibus Maximis, editio stereotypa, Ratisbonae, 1903.

Codex Iuris Canonici Pii X Pontificis Maximi iussu digestus Benedicti Papae XV auctoritate promulgatus, Romae: Typis Polyglottis Vaticanis, 1917. Reimpressio, 1934.

Codex Theodosianus, Krueger, P., Berolini: apud Weidmannos, 1923-1926.

Codicis Iuris Canonici Fontes cura Emi Petri Card. Gasparri editi, 9 vols., Romae [later Civitate Vaticana]: Typis Polyglottis Vaticanis, 1923-1939. (Vols. VII-IX *ed. cura et studio Emi Iustiniani Card. Serédi.*)

Collectanea S. Congregationis de Propaganda Fide, 2 vols., Romae: Typographia Polyglotta S. C. de Propaganda Fide, 1907.

Concilii Tridentini Diariorum, Actorum, Epistolarum Tractatuum, Nova Collectio, edidit Societas Gorresiana, 13 vols., Friburgi, Brisgoviae: B. Herder, 1911-1938.

Corpus Iuris Canonici, ed. Lipsien. 2, post Aemilii Ludovici Richteri curas instruxit Aemilus Fredberg, 2 vols., Lipsiae: Ex Officina Bernhardi Tauchnitz,1879-1881. Editio anastatice repetita, Lipsiae: Tauchnitz, 1922.

Corpus Scriptorum Ecclesiasticorum Latinorum, 68 vols., Vindobonae, 1866—

Decretales D. Gregorii Papae IX, Una Cum Glossis Restitutae, Romae, 1582.

Decretum Gratiani Emendatum et Notationibus Illustratum, Una Cum Glossis, Venetiis, 1605.

Hinschius, Paul, *Decretales Pseudo-Isidorianae et Capitula Angelramni,* Lipsiae: ex Officina Bernhardi Tauschnitz, 1863.

Iuliani Epitome Latina Novellarum Justiniani, Haenel, Gustavus, Lipsiae: prostat apud Hinrichsium, 1873.

Jaffé, Phillipus, *Regesta Pontificum Romanorum,* ed. secundam correctam et auctam auspiciis Gulielmi Wattenbach curaverunt F. Kaltenbrunner (ad annum 590), P. Ewald (anno 590-882), S. Löwenfeld (anno 882-1198) Lipsiae, 1885-1888.

Mansi, Ioannes, *Sacrorum Conciliorum Nova et Amplissima Collectio,* 53 vols. in 59, Paris, Arnhem, Leipzig, 1901-1927.

Monumenta Germaniae Historica, 188 vols., Hannoverae, 1826—*Legum Sectio II, Capitularia Regum Francorum,* tom. I, ed. A. Boretius, 1883.

Pallottini, Salvator, *Collectio Omnium Conclusionum et Resolutionum Quae in causis propositis apud Sacram Congregationem Cardinalium S. Concilii Tridentini Interpretum Prodierunt ab ejus institutione anno MDLXIV ad annum MDCCCLX, distinctis titulis alphabetico ordine per materias digesta,* 17 vols., Romae, 1868-1893.

Potthast, Augustus, *Regesta Pontificum Romanorum, inde ab A. post Christum natum MCXCVIII ad A. MCCCIV,* 2 vols., Berolini, 1874-1875.

Quinque Compilationes Antiquae, Aemilius Friedberg, Lipsiae, 1882.

Schroeder, Henry J., *Canons and Decrees of the Council of Trent,* St. Louis: Herder, 1941.

———, *Disciplinary Decrees of the General Councils: Text, Translation and Commentary,* St. Louis: Herder, 1937.

Thesaurus Resolutionum Sacrae Congregationis Concilii, 167 vols., Romae, 1718-1908.

Authors

Alford, Culver Bernard, *Jus Matrimoniale Comparatum,* New York: P. J. Kenedy & Sons, 1938.

Allègre, G., *Impedimentorum Matrimonii Synopsis,* 4. ed., Paris, 1889.

Andreucci, Andreas, *Hierarchia Ecclesiastica in Varias Suas Partes Distributa,* 2 vols., Romae: Generosus Salomonus, 1766.

Ayrinhac, H. A., *General Legislation in the New Code of Canon Law,* New York: Longmans, Green & Co., 1925.

———, *Legislation on the Sacraments in the New Code of Canon Law,* New York: Longmans, Green & Co., 1928.

Ayrinhac, H. A., and Lydon, R. J., *Marriage Legislation in the New Code of Canon Law,* revised ed., New York: Benziger Bros., Inc., 1940.

Benedictus XIV, *De Synodo Dioecesana,* 2 vols., Romae: Typographia S. C. de Propaganda Fide, 1806.

Beste, Udalricus, *Introductio in Codicem,* Collegeville, Minnesota: St. John's Abbey Press, 1938.

Blat, Albertus, *Commentarium Textus Codicis Iuris Canonici,* 5 vols. in 6, Romae: Collegio Angelico, 1921-1927.

Campagna, Angelo, *Il Vicario Generale del Vescovo,* The Catholic University of America Canon Law Studies, n. 66, Washington, D. C.: The Catholic University of America, 1931.

Cappello, Felix M., *Summa Iuris Canonici,* Vols. I-II, 2 ed., 1932-1934; Vol. III, 1936, Romae: apud Aedes Universitatis Gregorianae, 1932-1936.

———, *Tractatus Canonico-Moralis de Sacramentis,* Vol. III, *De Matrimonio,* ed. quarta emendata et aucta, Romae: apud Aedes Universitatis Gregorianae, 1939.

Carberry, John J., *The Juridical Form of Marriage,* The Catholic University of America Canon Law Studies, n. 84, Washington, D. C.: The Catholic University of America, 1934.

Chelodi, Ioannes, *Ius De Personis,* Tridenti: Libr. Edit. Tridentum, 1922.

———, *Ius Matrimoniale* ed. quarta, recognita et aucta a V. Dalpiaz, Tridenti: Libreria Moderna Editrice A. Ardesi, 1937.

Cicognani, Amleto, *Canon Law,* 2 revised edition, authorized English version by Jos. O'Hara and Francis Brennan, Philadelphia: The Dolphin Press, 1935.

Cocchi, Guidus, *Commentarium in Codicem Iuris Canonici,* 8 vols., Taurinorum Augustae: Marietti, 1931-1940. Vol. I, 5. ed., 1938; Vol. II, 4. ed., 1937; Vol. III, 3. ed., 1931; Vol. IV, 3. ed., 1932; Vol. V, 3. ed., 1932; Vol. VI, 3. ed., 1933; Vol. VII, 3. ed., 1940; Vol. VIII, 4. ed., 1938.

Connor, Maurice, *The Administrative Removal of Pastors,* The Catholic University of America Canon Law Studies, n. 104, Washington, D. C.: The Catholic University of America, 1937.

Coronata, Matthaeus, Conte a, *Institutiones Iuris Canonici,* 5 vols., Taurini, Romae: Marietti, 1933-1939. Vols. I-II, 2. ed., 1939; Vol. III, 1933; Vol. IV, 1935; Vol. V, 1936.

———, *Compendium Iuris Canonici,* 2 vols., Taurini: Marietti, 1937-1938.

Costello, John Michael, *Domicile and Quasi-Domicile,* The Catholic University of America Canon Law Studies, n. 60, Washington, D. C.: The Catholic University of America, 1930.

Davis, Henry, *Moral and Pastoral Theology,* Heythrop Series, n. 2, 3. ed., 4 vols., London: Sheed & Ward, 1938.

Dillon, Robert E., *Common Law Marriage,* The Catholic University of America Canon Law Studies, n. 153, Washington, D. C.: The Catholic University of America Press, 1942.

Doheny, William J., *Canonical Procedure in Matrimonial Cases,* Milwaukee: The Bruce Publishing Co., 1938.

Donovan, James J., *The Pastor's Obligation in Pre-Nuptial Investigation,* The Catholic University of America Canon Law Studies, n. 115, Washington, D. C.: The Catholic University of America, 1938.

Du Cange, Carolus Dufresne, *Glossarium Ad Scriptores Mediae et Infimae Latinitatis,* 6 vols., Parisiis, 1733.

Farrell, Benjamin F., *The Rights and Duties of the Local Ordinary Regarding Congregations of Women Religious of Pontifical Approval,* The Catholic University of America Canon Law Studies, n. 128, Washington, D. C.: The Catholic University of America Press, 1941.

Gasparri, Petrus, *Tractatus Canonicus de Matrimonio,* 3. ed., 2 vols., Parisiis, 1904.

———, *Tractatus Canonicus de Matrimonio,* ed nova, ad mentem Codicis I. C., 2 vols., Romae: Typis Polyglottis Vaticanis, 1932.

Genicot, Eduardus, et Salsmans, I., *Institutiones Iuris Theologiae Moralis,* 14. ed., 2 vols., Buenos Aires: Dedebec Ediciones Desclèe, De Brouwer, 1939.

Giraldi, Ubaldo, *Expositio Iuris Pontificii iuxta Recentiorem Ecclesiae Disciplinam,* nova Romana editio accuratior, Romae, Reimpressio, 1830.

Gonzalez-Tellez, Emmanuel, *Commentaria Perpetua in Singulos Textus quinque librorum Decretalium Gregorii IX,* 5 vols., Venetiis, 1699.

Hannan, Jerome D., *The Canon Law of Wills,* The Catholic University of America Canon Law Studies, n. 86, Washington, D. C.: The Catholic University of America, 1934.

Heston, Edward L., *The Alienation of Church Property in the United States,* The Catholic University of America Canon Law Studies, n. 132, Washington, D. C.: The Catholic University of America Press, 1941.

Hogan, James J., *Judicial Advocates and Procurators,* The Catholic University of America Canon Law Studies, n. 133, Washington, D. C.: The Catholic University of America Press, 1941.

Hostiensis, Cardinalis (Henricus de Segusia), *Summa Aurea,* Lugdoni, 1580.

Hughes, James A., *Witnesses in Criminal Trials of Clerics,* The Catholic University of America Canon Law Studies, n. 106, Washington, D. C.: The Catholic University of America, 1937.

Kearney, Raymond A., *The Principles of Delegation,* The Catholic University of America Canon Law Studies, n. 55, Washington, D. C.: The Catholic University of America, 1929.

Król, John J., *The Defendant in Contentious Trials,* The Catholic University of America Canon Law Studies, n. 146, Washington, D. C.: The Catholic University of America Press, 1942.

Kubelbeck, William J., *The Sacred Penitentiaria and Its Relations to Faculties of Ordinaries and Priests,* The Catholic University of America Canon Law Studies, n. 5, Washington, D. C.: The Catholic University of America, 1918.

Leage, R. W., *Roman Private Law,* 2. ed., London: Macmillan & Co., 1930.

Louis, William F., *Diocesan Archives,* The Catholic University of America Canon Law Studies, n. 137, Washington, D. C.: The Catholic University of America Press, 1941.

Maroto, P., *Institutiones Iuris Canonici ad Normam Novi Codicis,* 2 vols., Matriti, 1919-1921.

Mazzaeus, Franciscus, *De Matrimonio Conscientiae,* Romae, 1766.

McDevitt, Gilbert J., *Legitimacy and Legitimation,* The Catholic University of America Canon Law Studies, n. 138, Washington, D. C.: The Catholic University of America Press, 1941.

Merkelbach, Benedictus Henricus, *Summa Theologiae Moralis,* 2 ed., 3 vols., Parisiis: Typis Desclèe De Brouwer et Soc., 1936.

Michiels, Gommarus, *Normae Generales Iuris Canonici,* 2 vols., Lublin, Polonia: Universitas Catholica, 1929.

Migne, Jacques Paul, *Patrologiae Cursus Completus, Series Latina,* 221 vols., Parisiis, 1844-1864.

———, *Patrologiae Cursus Completus, Series Graeca,* 162 vols., Parisiis, 1856-1866.

Moriarty, Eugene J., *Oaths in Ecclesiastical Courts,* The Catholic University of America Canon Law Studies, n. 110, Washington, D. C.: The Catholic University of America, 1937.

Nau, Louis J., *Manual on the Marriage Laws of the Code of Canon Law,* 2 ed., Cincinnati: Frederick Pustet Co., Inc., 1934.

Noldin, H., et Schmitt, A., *Summa Theologiae Moralis,* 3 vols., Oeniponte: Typis et Sumptibus F. Rauch. Vol. I, 25 ed., 1937; vol. II, III, 24 ed., 1936.

O'Brien, Joseph D., *The Exemption of Religious in Church Law,* Milwaukee: The Bruce Publishing Co., 1942.

O'Neill, William H., *Papal Recripts of Favor,* The Catholic University of America Canon Law Studies, n. 57, Washington, D. C.: The Catholic University of America, 1930.

O'Rourke, James J., *Parish Registers,* The Catholic University of America Canon Law Studies, n. 88, Washington, D. C.: The Catholic University of America, 1934.

Ottaviani, Alaphridus, *Institutiones Iuris Publici Ecclesiastici,* 2 ed., 2 vols., [Civitate Vaticana:] Typis Polyglottis Vaticanis, 1935-1936.

Payen, G., *De Matrimonio in Missionibus et Potissimum in Sinis Tractatus Practicus et Casus,* 3 vols., Zi-ka-wei: In typographia T'ou-sè-wè, 1929.

Perugini, Angelus, *Concordata Vigentia Notis Historicis et Iuridicis Declarata,* Romae: apud custodiam librariam Pont. Instituti Utriusque Iuris S. Apollinare, 1934.

Petrovits, Joseph, J. C., *The New Church Law on Matrimony,* Philadelphia: John J. McVey, 1921.

Pirhing, Henricus, *Ius Canonicum Nova Methodo Explicatum,* ed. novissima, 5 vols., Dilingae, 1728.

Quigley, Joseph, A. M., *A Summary of the Canon Law on Matrimonial Impediments and Dispensations,* 2 ed., Philadelphia: The Dolphin Press, 1942.

Regan, Robert E., *Professional Secrecy in the Light of Moral Principles,* Washington, D. C.: Augustinian Press, 1943.

Reiffenstuel, Anacletus, *Ius Canonicum Universum,* 4 vols., Venetiis, 1735.

Reilly, Edward M., *The General Norms of Dispensation,* The Catholic University of America Canon Law Studies, n. 119, Washington, D. C.: The Catholic University of America Press, 1939.

Roberts, James B., *The Banns of Marriage,* The Catholic University of America Canon Law Studies, n. 64, Washington, D. C.: The Catholic University of America, 1931.

Rossi, Josephus, *De Matrimonio Celebratione Iuxta Codicem Iuris Canonici,* Romae: Fredericus Pustet, 1924.

Sanchez, Thoma, *Tres Libri De Sancto Matrimonii Sacramento Disputationum,* Antwerpiae, 1626.

Santi, Franciscus, *Praelectiones Iuris Canonici,* 2 ed., 5 vols., Ratisbonae: F. Pustet, 1892.

Schmalzgrueber, Franciscus, *Ius Ecclesiasticum Universum,* 5 vols. in 12, Romae, 1843-1845.

Van Hove, A., *Prolegomena Codicem Iuris Canonici,* Mechliniae: H. Dessain, 1928.

Vermeersch, Arthurus, *Theologiae Moralis, Principia—Responsa—Consilia,* 3 ed., 3 vols., Romae: Universita Gregoriana, 1933-1937.

Vermeersch, A., et Creusen, J., *Epitome Iuris Canonici,* 3 vols., Mechliniae-Romae: H. Dessain, 1934-1937. Vol. I, 6 ed., 1937; vols. II, III, 5 ed., 1934-1936.

Vlaming, T. M. *Praelectiones Iuris Matrimonii Ad Norman Codicis Iuris Canonici,* 3 ed., 2 vols., Bussum in Hollandia: Sumptibus Societatis Editricis Anonymae Olim Paulus Brand, 1921.

Wernz, Franciscus X., *Ius Decretalium,* 6 vols., Romae et Prati, 1898-1905.

Wernz, Franciscus, et Vidal, Petrus, *Ius Canonicum ad Codicis Normam Exactum,* 7 vols. in 8, Romae: apud Aedes Universitatis Gregorianae, 1923-1938. Vol. V, *Ius Matrimoniale,* 2. ed., 1928.

Woywod, Stanislaus, *A Practical Commentary on the Code of Canon Law,* 2 vols., New York: Joseph F. Wagner, Inc., 1925.

Zitelli-Natali, Zephyrinus, *Apparatus Iuris Ecclesiastici,* Romae: Ex Typis Soc. Edit. Rom., 1886.

Perodicals

Apollinaris, Romae, 1928—

Archiv für katholisches Kirchenrecht, Vols. I-VI (1857-1861), Innsbruck; Vols. VI— (1862-), Mainz.

Jurist, The, Washington, D. C., 1941—

Articles

Hilling, Nicolaus, "Eherectliche Kontroversen und Probleme",—*AKKR,* CV (1925), 108-111.

Roelker, Edward, "The Vicar General and the Special Mandate",—*The Jurist,* II (1942), 346-362.

ABBREVIATIONS

AAS—*Acta Apostolicae Sedis.*
AKKR—*Archiv für katholisches Kirchenrecht.*
ASS—*Acta Sanctae Sedis.*
Coll. Lac.—*Collectio Lacensis.*
Coll. S. C. P. F.—*Collectanea S. C. de Propaganda Fide.*
Fontes—*Codicis Iuris Canonici Fontes cura . . . Gasparri editi.*
JE—Jaffé, *Regesta Pontificum Romanorum* (edited by Ewald, from 590-882).
JK—Jaffé, *op. cit.* (*edited by Kaltenbrunner,* from 0-590).
JL—Jaffé, *op. cit.* (edited by Loewenfeld, from 882-1198).
Pallottini—Pallottini, *Collectio . . . S. C. C.*
S. C. C.—Sacra Congregatio Concilii.
S. C. de Prop. Fide—Sacra Congregatio de Propaganda Fide.
S. C. de Sacr.—Sacra Congregatio de Disciplina Sacramentorum.
S. C. pro Eccl. Orient.—Sacra Congregatio pro Ecclesia Orientali.

ALPHABETICAL INDEX

BIOGRAPHICAL NOTE

VINCENT PAUL COBURN was born September 10, 1915, in Newark, New Jersey. He obtained his elementary education at St. Rose of Lima Parochial School in Newark, and completed his secondary education at Seton High School, South Orange, New Jersey. He pursued his college studies at Seton Hall College, from which institution he received the Degree of Bachelor of Arts in June 1937. On September 10, 1936, he entered the Immaculate Conception Seminary, Darlington, New Jersey, and was ordained to the Sacred Priesthood June 7, 1941. He entered the School of Canon Law at the Catholic University of America in September 1941. From this institution he received the degrees of the Baccalaureate in Canon Law in May, 1942, and of the Licentiate in Canon Law in May, 1943.

CANON LAW STUDIES *

1. FRERIKS, REV. CELESTINE A., C.PP.S., J.C.D., Religious Congregations in Their External Relations, 121 pp., 1916.
2. GALLAGHER, REV. DANIEL M., O.P., J.C.D., Canonical Elections, 117 pp., 1917.
3. BORKOWSKI, REV. AURELIUS L., O.F.M., J.C.D., De Confraternitatibus Ecclesiasticis, 136 pp., 1918.
4. CASTILLO, REV. CAYO, J.C.D., Disertacion Historico-Canonica sobre la Potestad del Cabildo en Sede Vacante o Impedida del Vicario Capitular, 99 pp., 1919 (1918).
5. KUBELBECK, REV. WILLIAM J., S.T.B., J.C.D., The Sacred Penitentiaria and Its Relation to Faculties of Ordinaries and Priests, 129 pp., 1918.
6. PETROVITS, REV. JOSEPH, J.C., S.T.D., J.C.D., The New Church Law on Matrimony, X-461 pp., 1919.
7. HICKEY, REV. JOHN J., S.T.B., J.C.D., Irregularities and Simple Impediments in the New Code of Canon Law, 100 pp., 1920.
8. KLEKOTKA, REV. PETER J., S.T.B., J.C.D., Diocesan Consultors, 179 pp., 1920.
9. WANENMACHER, REV. FRANCIS, J.C.D., The Evidence in Ecclesiastical Procedure Affecting the Marriage Bond, 1920 (Printed 1935).
10. GOLDEN, REV. HENRY FRANCIS, J.C.D., Parochial Benefices in the New Code, IV-119 pp., 1921 (Printed 1925).
11. KOUDELKA, REV. CHARLES J., J.C.D., Pastors, Their Rights and Duties According to the New Code of Canon Law, 211 pp., 1921.
12. MELO, REV. ANTONIUS, O.F.M., J.C.D., De Exemptione Regularium, X-188 pp., 1921.
13. SCHAFF, REV. VALENTINE THEODORE, O.F.M., S.T.B., J.C.D., The Cloister, X-180 pp., 1921.
14. BURKE, REV. THOMAS JOSEPH, S.T.D., J.C.D., Competence in Ecclesiastical Tribunals, IV-117 pp., 1922.
15. LEECH, REV. GEORGE LEO, J.C.D., A. Compartive Study of the Constitution "Apostolicae Sedis" and the "Codex Juris Canonici," 179 pp., 1922.
16. MOTRY, REV. HUBERT LOUIS, S.T.D., J.C.D., Diocesan Faculties According to the Code of Canon Law, II-167 pp., 1922.

* Below n. 100 only the following numbers are still available: Nn. 3, 4, 9, 25, 34, 57 and 75. Beginning with n. 100 only the following are available: Nn. 100-111 inclusive, and n. 113.

17. MURPHY, REV. GEORGE LAWRENCE, J.C.D., Delinquencies and Penalties in the Administration and the Reception of the Sacraments, IV-121 pp., 1923.
18. O'REILLY, REV. JOHN ANTHONY, S.T.B., J.C.D., Ecclesiastical Sepulture in the New Code of Canon Law, II-129 pp., 1923.
19. MICHALICKA, REV. WENCESLAS CYRILL, O.S.B., J.C.D., Judicial Procedure in Dismissal of Clerical Exempt Religious, 107 pp., 1923.
20. DARGIN, REV. EDWARD VINCENT, S.T.B., J.C.D., Reserved Cases According to the Code of Canon Law, IV-103 pp., 1924.
21. GODFREY, REV. JOHN A., S.T.B., J.C.D., The Right of Patronage According to the Code of Canon Law, 153 pp., 1924.
22. HAGEDORN, REV. FRANCIS EDWARD, J.C.D., General Legislation on Indulgences, II-154 pp., 1924.
23. KING, REV. JAMES IGNATIUS, J.C.D., The Administration of the Sacraments to Dying Non-Catholics, V-141 pp., 1924.
24. WINSLOW, REV. FRANCIS JOSEPH, O.F.M., J.C.D., Vicars and Prefects Apostolic, IV-149 pp., 1924.
25. CORREA, REV. JOSE SERVELION, S.T.L., J.C.D., La Potestad Legislativa de la Iglesia Catolica, IV-127 pp., 1925.
26. DUGAN, REV. HENRY FRANCIS, A.M., J.C.D., The Judiciary Department of the Diocesan Curia, 87 pp., 1925.
27. KELLER, REV. CHARLES FREDERICK, S.T.B., J.C.D., Mass Stipends, 167 pp., 1925.
28. PASCHANG, REV. JOHN LINUS, J.C.D., The Sacramentals According to the Code of Canon Law, 129 pp., 1925.
29. PIONTEK, REV. CYRILLUS, O.F.M., S.T.B., J.C.D., De Indulto Exclaustrationis necnon Saecularizationis, XIII-289 pp., 1925.
30. KEARNEY, REV. RICHARD JOSEPH, S.T.B., J.C.D., Sponsors at Baptism According to the Code of Canon Law, IV-127 pp., 1925.
31. BARTLETT, REV. CHESTER JOSEPH, A.M., LL.B., J.C.D., The Tenure of Parochial Property in the United States of America, V-108 pp., 1926.
32. KILKER, REV. ADRIAN JEROME, J.C.D., Extreme Unction, V-425 pp., 1926.
33. MCCORMICK, REV. ROBERT EMMETT, J.C.D., Confessors of Religious, VIII-266 pp., 1926.
34. MILLER, REV. NEWTON THOMAS, J.C.D., Founded Masses According to the Code of Canon Law, VII-93 pp., 1926.
35. ROELKER, REV. EDWARD G., S.T.D., J.C.D., Principles of Privilege According to the Code of Canon Law, XI-166 pp., 1926.
36. BAKALARCZYK, REV. RICHARDUS, M.I.C., J.U.D., De Novitiatu, VIII-208 pp., 1927.
37. PIZZUTI, REV. LAWRENCE, O.F.M., J.U.L., De Parochis Religiosis, 1927. (Not Printed.)

38. BLILEY, REV. NICHOLAS MARTIN, O.S.B., J.C.D., Altars According to the Code of Canon Law, XIX-132 pp., 1927.
39. BROWN, MR. BRENDAN FRANCIS, A.B., LL.M., J.U.D. The Canonical Juristic Personality with Special Reference to its Status in the United States of America, V-212 pp., 1927.
40. CAVANAUGH, REV. WILLIAM THOMAS, C.P., J.U.D., The Reservation of the Blessed Sacrament, VIII-101 pp., 1927.
41. DOHENY, REV. WILLIAM J., C.S.C., A.B., J.U.D. Church Property: Modes of Acquisition, X-118 pp., 1927.
42. FELDHAUS, REV. ALOYSIUS H., C.PP.S., J.C.D., Oratories, IX-141 pp., 1927.
43. KELLY, REV. JAMES PATRICK, A.B., J.C.D., The Jurisdiction of the Simple Confessor, X-208 pp., 1927.
44. NEUBERGER, REV. NICHOLAS J., J.C.D., Canon 6 or the Relation of the Codex Juris Canonici to the Preceding Legislation, V-95 pp., 1927.
45. O'KEEFE, REV. GERALD MICHAEL, J.C.D., Matrimonial Dispensations, Powers of Bishops, Priests, and Confessors, VIII-232 pp., 1927.
46. QUIGLEY, REV. JOSEPH A. M., A.B., J.C.D., Condemned Societies, 139 pp., 1927.
47. ZAPLOTNIK, REV. JOHANNES LEO, J.C.D., De Vicariis Foraneis, X-142 pp., 1927.
48. DUSKIE, REV. JOHN ALOYSIUS, A.B., J.C.D., The Canonical Status of the Orientals in the United States, VIII-196 pp., 1928.
49. HYLAND, REV. FRANCIS EDWARD, J.C.D., Excommunication, Its Nature, Historical Development and Effects, VIII-181 pp., 1928.
50. REINMANN, REV. GERALD JOSEPH, O.M.C., J.C.D., The Third Order Secular of Saint Francis, 201 pp., 1928.
51. SCHENK, REV. FRANCIS J., J.C.D., The Matrimonial Impediments of Mixed Religion and Disparity of Cult, XVI-318 pp., 1929.
52. COADY, REV. JOHN JOSEPH, S.T.D., J.U.D., A.M., The Appointment of Pastors, VIII-150 pp., 1929.
53. KAY, REV. THOMAS HENRY, J.C.D., Competence in Matrimonial Procedure, VIII-164 pp., 1929.
54. TURNER, REV. SIDNEY JOSEPH, C.P., J.U.D., The Vow of Poverty, XLIX-217 pp., 1929.
55. KEARNEY, REV. RAYMOND A., A.B., S.T.D., J.C.D., The Principles of Delegation, VII-149 pp., 1929.
56. CONRAN, REV. EDWARD JAMES, A.B., J.C.D., The Interdict, V-163 pp., 1930.
57. O'NEILL, REV. WILLIAM H., J.C.D., Papal Rescripts of Favor, VII-218 pp., 1930.
58. BASTNAGEL, REV. CLEMENT VINCENT, J.U.D., The Appointment of Parochial Adjutants and Assistants, XV-257 pp., 1930.
59. FERRY, REV. WILLIAM A., A.B., J.C.D., Stole Fees, V-136 pp., 1930.

60. Costello, Rev. John Michael, A.B., J.C.D., Domicile and Quasi-Domicile, VII-201 pp., 1930.
61. Kremer, Rev. Michael Nicholas, A.B., S.T.B., J.C.D., Church Support in the United States, VI-136 pp., 1930.
62. Angulo, Rev. Luis, C.M., J.C.D., Legislation de la Iglesia sobre la intencion en la application de la Santa Misa, VII-104 pp., 1931.
63. Frey, Rev. Wolfgang Norbert, O.S.B., A.B., J.C.D., The Act of Religious Profession, VIII-174 pp., 1931.
64. Roberts, Rev. James Brendan, A.B., J.C.D., The Banns of Marriage, XIV-140 pp., 1931.
65. Ryder, Rev. Raymond Aloysius, A.B., J.C.D., Simony, IX-151 pp., 1931.
66. Campagna, Rev. Angelo, Ph.D., J.U.D., Il Vicario Generale del Vescovo, VII-205 pp., 1931.
67. Cox, Rev. Joseph Godfrey, A.B., J.C.D., The Administration of Seminaries, VI-124 pp., 1931.
68. Gregory, Rev. Donald J., J.U.D., The Pauline Privilege, XV-165 pp., 1931.
69. Donohue, Rev. John F., J.C.D., The Impediment of Crime, VII-110 pp., 1931.
70. Dooley, Rev. Eugene A., O.M.I., J.C.D., Church Law on Sacred Relics, IX-143 pp., 1931.
71. Orth, Rev. Clement Raymond, O.M.C., J.C.D., The Approbation of Religious Institutes, 171 pp., 1931.
72. Pernicone, Rev. Joseph M., A.B., J.C.D., The Ecclesiastical Prohibition of Books, XII-267 pp., 1932.
73. Clinton, Rev. Connell, A.B., J.C.D., The Paschal Precept, IX-108 pp., 1932.
74. Donnelly, Rev. Francis B., A.M., S.T.L., J.C.D., The Diocesan Synod, VIII-125 pp., 1932.
75. Torrente, Rev. Camilo, C.M.F., J.C.D., Las Processiones Sagradas, V-145 pp., 1932.
76. Murphy, Rev. Edwin J., C.PP.S., J.C.D., Suspension Ex Informata Conscientia, XI-122 pp., 1932.
77. MacKenzie, Rev. Eric F., A.M., S.T.L., J.C.D., The Delict of Heresy in its Commission, Penalization, Absolution, VII-124 pp., 1932.
78. Lyons, Rev. Avitus E., S.T.B., J.C.D., The Collegiate Tribunal of First Instance, XI-147 pp., 1932.
79. Connolly, Rev. Thomas A., J.C.D., Appeals, XI-195 pp., 1932.
80. Sangmeister, Rev. Joseph V., A.B., J.C.D., Force and Fear as Precluding Matrimonial Consent, V-211 pp., 1932.
81. Jaeger, Rev. Leo A., A.B., J.C.D., The Administration of Vacant and Quasi-Vacant Episcopal Sees in the United States, IX-299 pp., 1932.
82. Rimlinger, Rev. Herbert T., J.C.D., Error Invalidating Matrimonial Consent, VII-79 pp., 1932.

83. Barrett, Rev. John D. M., S.S., J.C.D., A Comparative Study of the Third Plenary Council of Baltimore and the Code, IX-221 pp., 1932.
84. Carberry, Rev. John J., Ph.D., S.T.D., J.C.D., The Juridical Form of Marriage, X-177 pp., 1934.
85. Dolan, Rev. John L., A.B., J.C.D., The Defensor Vinculi, XII-157 pp., 1934.
86. Hannan, Rev. Jerome D., A.M., S.T.D., LL.B., J.C.D., The Canon Law of Wills, IX-517 pp., 1934.
87. Lemieux, Rev. Delise A., A.M., J.C.D., The Sentence in Ecclesiastical Procedure, IX-131 pp., 1934.
88. O'Rourke, Rev. James J., A.B., J.C.D., Parish Registers, VII-109 pp., 1934.
89. Timlin, Rev. Bartholomew, O.F.M., A.M., J.C.D., Conditional Matrimonial Consent, X-381 pp., 1934.
90. Wahl, Rev. Francis X., A.B., J.C.D., The Matrimonial Impediments of Consanguinity and Affinity, VI-125 pp., 1934.
91. White, Rev. Robert J., A.B., LL.B., S.T.B., J.C.D., Canonical Ante-Nuptial Promises and the Civil Law, VI-152 pp., 1934.
92. Herrera, Rev. Antonio Parra, O.C.D., J.C.D., Legislation Ecclesiastica sobra el Ayuno y la Abstinencia, XI-191 pp., 1935.
93. Kennedy, Rev. Edwin J., J.C.D., The Special Matrimonial Process in Cases of Evident Nullity, X-165 pp., 1935.
94. Manning, Rev. John J., A.B., J.C.D., Presumption of Law in Matrimonial Procedure, XI-111 pp., 1935.
95. Moeder, Rev. John M., J.C.D., The Proper Bishop for Ordination and Dismissorial Letters, VII-135 pp., 1935.
96. O'Mara, Rev. William A., A.B., J.C.D., Canonical Causes for Matrimonial Dispensations, IX-155 pp., 1935.
97. Reilly, Rev. Peter, J.C.D., Residence of Pastors, IX-81 pp., 1935.
98. Smith, Rev. Mariner T., O.P., S.T.Lr., J.C.D., The Penal Law for Religious, VIII-169 pp., 1935.
99. Whalen, Rev. Donald W., A.M.,J.C.D., The Value of Testimonial Evidence in Matrimonial Procedure, XIII-297 pp., 1935.
100. Cleary, Rev. Joseph F., J.C.D., Canonical Limitations on the Alienation of Church Property, VIII-141 pp., 1936.
101. Glynn, Rev. John C., J.C.D., The Promoter of Justice, XX-337 pp., 1936.
102. Brennan, Rev. James H., S.S., M.A., S.T.B., J.C.D., The Simple Convalidation of Marriage, VI-135 pp., 1937.
103. Brunini, Rev. Joseph Bernard, J.C.D., The Clerical Obligations of Canons 139 and 142, X-121 pp., 1937.
104. Connor, Rev. Maurice, A.B., J.C.D., The Administrative Removal of Pastors, VIII-159 pp., 1937.
105. Guilfoyle, Rev. Merlin Joseph, J.C.D., Custom, XI-144 pp., 1937.

106. Hughes, Rev. James Austin, A.B., A.M., J.C.D., Witnesses in Criminal Trials of Clerics, IX-140 pp., 1937.
107. Jansen, Rev. Raymond J., A.B., S.T.L., J.C.D., Canonical Provisions for Catechetical Instruction, VII-153 pp., 1937.
108. Kealy, Rev. John James, A.B., J.C.D., The Introductory Libellus in Church Court Procedure, XI-121 pp., 1937.
109. McManus, Rev. James Edward, C.SS.R., J.C.D., The Administration of Temporal Goods in Religious Institutes, XVI-196 pp., 1937.
110. Moriarty, Rev. Eugene James, J.C.D., Oaths in Ecclesiastical Courts, X-115 pp., 1937.
111. Rainier, Rev. Eligius George, C.SS.R., J.C.D., Suspension of Clerics, XVII-249 pp., 1937.
112. Reilly, Rev. Thomas F., C.SS.R., J.C.D., Visitation of Religious, VI-195 pp., 1938.
113. Moriarty, Rev. Francis E., C.SS.R., J.C.D., The Extraordinary Absolution from Censures, XV-334 pp., 1938.
114. Connolly, Rev. Nicholas P., J.C.D., The Canonical Erection of Parishes, X-132 pp., 1938.
115. Donovan, Rev. James Joseph, J.C.D., The Pastor's Obligation in Pre-nuptial Investigation, XII-322 pp., 1938.
116. Harrigan, Rev. Robert J., M.A., S.T.B., J.C.D., The Radical Sanation of Invalid Marriages, VIII-208 pp., 1938.
117. Boffa, Rev. Conrad Humbert, J.C.D., Canonical Provisions for Catholic Schools, VII-211 pp., 1939.
118. Parsons, Rev. Anscar John, O.M.Cap., J.C.D., Canonical Elections, XII-236 pp., 1939.
119. Reilly, Rev. Edward Michael, A.B., J.C.D., The General Norms of Dispensation, XII-156 pp., 1939.
120. Ryan, Rev. Gerald Aloysius, A.B., J.C.D., Principles of Episcopal Jurisdiction, XII-172 pp., 1939.
121. Burton, Rev. Francis James, C.S.C., A.B., J.C.D., A Commentary on Canon 1125, X-222 pp., 1940.
122. Miaskiewicz, Rev. Francis Sigismund, J.C.D., Supplied Jurisdiction According to Canon 209, XII-340 pp., 1940.
123. Rice, Rev. Patrick William, A.B., J.C.D., Proof of Death in Pre-nuptial Investigation, VIII-156 pp., 1940.
124. Anglin, Rev. Thomas Francis, M.S., J.C.D., The Eucharistic Fast, VIII-183 pp., 1941.
125. Coleman, Rev. John Jerome, J.C.D., The Minister of Confirmation, VI-153 pp., 1941.
126. Downs, Rev. Joseph Emmanuel, A.B., J.C.D., The Concept of Clerical Immunity, XI-163 pp., 1941.
127. Esswein, Rev. Anthony Albert, J.C.D., Extrajudicial Penal Powers of Ecclesiastical Superiors, X-144 pp., 1941.

128. FARRELL, REV. BENJAMIN FRANCIS, M.A., S.T.L., J.C.D., The Rights and Duties of the Local Ordinary Regarding Congregations of Women Religious of Pontifical Approval, V-195 pp., 1941.
129. FEENEY, REV. THOMAS JOHN, A.B., S.T.L., J.C.D., Restitutio in Integrum, VI-169 pp., 1941.
130. FINDLAY, REV. STEPHEN WILLIAM, O.S.B., A.B., J.C.D., Canonical Norms Governing the Deposition and Degradation of Clerics, XVII-279 pp., 1941.
131. GOODWINE, REV. JOHN, A.B., S.T.L., J.C.D., The Right of the Church to Acquire Property, VIII-119 pp., 1941.
132. HESTON, REV. EDWARD LOUIS, C.S.C., PH.D., S.T.D., J.C.D., The Alienation of Church Property in the United States, XII-222 pp., 1941.
133. HOGAN, REV. JAMES JOHN, A.B., S.T.L., J.C.D., Judicial Advocates and Procurators, XIII-200 pp., 1941.
134. KEALY, REV. THOMAS M., A.B., Litt.B., J.C.D., Dowry of Women Religious, IX-152 pp., 1941.
135. KEENE, REV. MICHAEL JAMES, O.S.B., J.C.D., Religious Ordinaries and Canon 198, V-164 pp., 1942.
136. KERIN, REV. CHARLES A., S.S., M.A., S.T.B., J.C.D., The Privation of Christian Burial, XVI-279 pp., 1941.
137. LOUIS, REV. WILLIAM FRANCIS, M.A., J.C.D., Diocesan Archives, X-101 pp., 1941.
138. MCDEVITT, REV. GILBERT JOSEPH, A.B., J.C.D., Legitimacy and Legitimation, X-247 pp., 1941.
139. MCDONOUGH, REV. THOMAS JOSEPH, A.B., J.C.D., Apostolic Administrators, X-217 pp., 1941.
140. MEIER, REV. CARD ANTHONY, A.B., J.C.D., Penal Administrative Procedure Against Negligent Pastors, X-240 pp., 1941.
141. SCHMIDT, REV. JOHN ROGG, A.B., J.C.D., The Principles of Authentic Interpretation in Canon 17 of the Code of Canon Law, XII-331 pp., 1941.
142. SLAFKOSKY, REV. ANDREW LEONARD, A.B., J.C.D., The Canonical Episcopal Visitation of the Diocese, X-197 pp., 1941.
143. SWOBODA, REV. INNOCENT ROBERT, O.F.M., J.C.D., Ignorance in Relation to the Imputability of Delicts, IX-271 pp., 1941.
144. DUBE, REV. ARTHUR JOSEPH, A.B., J.C.D., The General Principles for the Reckoning of Time in Canon Law, VIII-299 pp., 1941.
145. MCBRIDE, REV. JAMES T., A.B., J.C.D., Incardinntion and Excardination of Seculars, XX-585 pp., 1941.
146. KRÓL, REV. JOHN T., J.C.D., The Defendant in Ecclesiastical Trials, XII-207 pp., 1942.
147. COMYNS, REV. JOSEPH J. C.SS.R., A.B., J.C.D., Papal and Episcopal Administration of Church Property, XIV-155 pp., 1942.

148. BARRY, REV. GARRETT FRANCIS, O.M.I., J.C.D., Violation of the Cloister, XII-260 pp., 1942.
149. BOLDUC, REV. GATIEN, C.S.V., A.B., S.T.L., J.C.D., Les Études dans les Religions Cléricales, VIII-155 pp., 1942.
150. BOYLE, REV. DAVID JOHN, M.A., J.C.D., The Juridic Effects of Moral Certitude on Pre-Nuptial Guarantees, XII-188 pp., 1942.
151. CANAVAN, REV. WALTER JOSEPH, M.A., LITT.D., J.C.D., The Profession of Faith, XII-143 pp., 1942.
152. DESROCHERS, REV. BRUNO, A.B., PH.L., S.T.B., J.C.D., Le Premier Concile Plénier de Québec et le Code de Droit Canonique, XIV-186 pp., 1942.
153. DILLON, REV. ROBERT EDWARD, A.B., J.C.D., Common Law Marriage, X-148 pp., 1942.
154. DODWELL, REV. EDWARD JOHN, PH.D., S.T.B., J.C.D., The Time and Place for the Celebration of Marriage, X-156 pp., 1942.
155. DONNELLAN, REV. THOMAS ANDREW, A.B., J.C.D., The Obligation of the Missa pro Populo, VII-131 pp., 1942.
156. ELTZ, REV. LOUIS ANTHONY, A.B., J.C.L., Cooperation in Crime.
157. GASS, REV. SYLVESTER FRANCIS, M.A., J.C.D., Ecclesiastical Pensions, XI-206 pp., 1942.
158. GUINIVEN, REV. JOHN JOSEPH, C.SS.R., J.C.D., The Precept of Hearing Mass, XIV-188 pp., 1942.
159. GULCZYNSKI, REV. JOHN THEOPHILUS, J.C.D., The Desecration and Violation of Churches, X-126 pp., 1942.
160. HAMMILL, REV. JOHN LEO, M.A., J.C.D., The Obligations of the Traveler According to Canon 14, VIII-204 pp., 1942.
161. HAYDT, REV. JOHN JOSEPH, A.B., J.C.D., Reserved Benefices, XI-148 pp., 1942.
162. HUSER, REV. ROGER JOHN, O.F.M., A.B., J.C.D., The Crime of Abortion in Canon Law, XII-187 pp., 1942.
163. KEARNEY, REV. FRANCIS PATRICK, A.B., S.T.L., J.C.L., The Principles of Canon 1127.
164. LINAHEN, REV. LEO JAMES, S.T.L., J.C.D., De Absolutione Complicis In Peccato Turpi, 114 pp., 1942.
165. McCLOSKEY, REV. JOSEPH ALOYSIUS, A.B., J.C.D., The Subject of Ecclesiastical Law According to Canon 12, XVII-246 pp., 1942.
166. O'NEILL, REV. FRANCIS JOSEPH, C.SS.R., J.C.D., The Dismissal of Religious in Temporary Vows, XIII-220 pp., 1942.
167. PRINCE, REV. JOHN EDWARD, A.B., S.T.B., J.C.D., The Diocesan Chancellor, X-136 pp., 1942.
168. RIESNER, REV. ALBERT JOSEPH, C.SS.R., J.C.D., Apostates and Fugitives from Religious Institutes, IX-168 pp., 1942.
169. STENGER, REV. JOSEPH BERNHARD, J.C.D., The Mortgaging of Church Property, 186 pp., 1942.

170. WALDRON, REV. JOSEPH FRANCIS, A.B., J.C.D., The Minister of Baptism, XII-197 pp., 1942.
171. WILLETT, REV. ROBERT ALBERT, J.C.D., The Probative Value of Documents in Ecclesiastical Trials, X-124 pp., 1942.
172. WOEBER, REV. EDWARD MARTIN, M.A., J.C.D., The Interpellations, XII-161 pp., 1942.
173. BENKO, REV. MATTHEW ALOYSIUS, O.S.B., M.A., J.C.L., The Abbot *Nullius.*
174. CHRIST, REV. JOSEPH JAMES, M.A., S.T.L., J.C.D., Dispensation from Vindicative Penalties, XIII-285 pp., 1943.
175. CLANCY, REV. PATRICK M. J., O.P., A.B., S.T.LR., J.C.D., The Local Religious Superior, X-229 pp., 1943.
176. CLARKE, REV. THOMAS JAMES, J.C.D., Parish Societies, XII-147 pp., 1943.
177. CONNOLLY, REV. JOHN PATRICK, S.T.L., J.C.D., Synodal Examiners and Parish Priest Consultors, X-223 pp., 1943.
178. DRUMM, REV. WILLIAM MARTIN, A.B., J.C.L., Hospital Chaplains.
179. FLANAGAN, REV. BERNARD JOSEPH, A.B., S.T.L., J.C.D., The Canonical Erection of Religious House, X-147 pp., 1943.
180. KELLEHER, REV. STEPHEN JOSEPH, A.B., S.T.B., J.C.D., Discussions with Non-Catholics: Canonical Legislation, X-93 pp., 1943.
181. LEWIS, REV. GORDIAN, C.P., J.C.D., Chapters in Religious Institutes, XII-169 pp., 1943.
182. MARX, REV. ADOLPH, J.C.D., The Declaration of Nullity of Marriages Contracted Outside the Church, X-151 pp., 1943.
183. MATULENAS, REV. RAYMOND ANTHONY, O.S.B., A.B., J.C.L., Communication, a Source of Privileges.
184. O'LEARY, REV. CHARLES GERARD, C.SS.R., Religious Dismissed After Perpetual Profession.
185. POWER, REV. CORNELIUS MICHAEL, J.C.L., The Blessing of Cemeteries.
186. SHUHLER, REV. RALPH VINCENT, O.S.A., J.C.D., Privileges of Religious to Absolve and Dispense, XII-195 pp., 1943.
187. ZIOLKOWSKI, REV. THADDEUS STANISLAUS, A.B., J.C.D., The Consecration and Blessing of Churches, XII-151 pp., 1943.
188. HENEGAN, REV. JOHN JOSEPH, S.T.D., J.C.D., The Marriages of Unworthy Catholics: Canons 1065 and 1066; XV-213 pp., 1944.
189. CARROLL, REV. COLEMAN FRANCIS, M.A., S.T.L., J.C.L., Charitable Institutions.
190. CIESLUK, REV. JOSEPH EDWARD, PH.B., S.T.L., J.C.L., National Parishes in the United States.
191. COBURN, REV. VINCENT PAUL, A.B., J.C.L., Marriages of Conscience.
192. CONNORS, REV. CHARLES PAUL, C.S.SP., A.B. J.C.D., Extra-Judicial Procurators in the Code of Canon Law, X-94 pp., 1944.
193. COYLE, REV. PAUL RAYMOND, A.B., J.C.L., Judicial Exceptions.

194. Fair, Rev. Bartholomew Francis, A.B., S.T.L., J.C.L., The Impediment of Abduction.
195. Gallagher, Rev. Thomas Raphael, O.P., A.B., S.T.Lr., J.C.L., The Examination of the Qualities of the Ordinand.
196. Gannon, Rev. John Mark, S.T.L., J.C.L., The Interstices Required for the Promotion to Orders.
197. Goldsmith, Rev. J. William, B.C.S., S.T.L., J.C.L., The Competence of Church and State over Marriage — Disputed Points.
198. Goodwine, Rev. Joseph Gerard, A.B., S.T.B., J.C.D., The Reception of Converts, XIII-326 pp., 1944.
199. Kowalsky, Rev. Romuald Eugene, O.F.M., A.B., J.C.L., Sustenance of Religious Houses of Regulars.
200. McCoy, Rev. Alan Edward, O.F.M., J.C.L., Force and Fear in Relation to Delictual Imputability and Penal Responsibility.
201. McDevitt, Rev. Vincent John, Ph.B., S.T.L., J.C.L., Perjury.
202. Martin, Rev. Thomas Owen, Ph.D., S.T.D., J.C.L., Adverse Possession, Prescription and Limitation of Actions: The Canonical "Praescriptio".
203. Miklosovic, Rev. Paul John, A.B., J.C.L., Attempted Marriages and their Consequent Juridic Effects.
204. Mundy, Rev. Thomas Maurice, A.B., S.T.L., J.C.L., The Union of Parishes.
205. O'Dea, Rev. John Coyle, A.B., J.C.L., The Matrimonial Impediment of Nonage.
206. Olalia, Rev. Alexander Ayson, S.T.L., J.C.L., A Comparative Study of the Christian Constitution of States and the Constitution of the Philippine Commonwealth.
207. Poisson, Rev. Pierre-Marie, C.S.C., A.B., Ph.L., Th.L., J.C.L., Droits Patrimoniaux des Maisons et des Eglises Religieuses.
208. Stadalnikas, Rev. Casimir Joseph, M.I.C., J.C.L., Reservation of Censures.
209. Sullivan, Rev. Eugene Henry, S.T.L., J.C.L., Proof of the Reception of the Sacraments.
210. Vaughan, Rev. William Edward, J.C.D., Constitutions for Diocesan Courts, X-210 pp., 1944.
211. Lyons, Rev. Joseph Henry, J.C.L., The Joinder of Issue in Canonical Trials.

www.ingramcontent.com/pod-product-compliance
Lightning Source LLC
LaVergne TN
LVHW050231080826
844660LV00012B/515

* 9 7 8 0 8 1 3 2 2 3 7 8 0 *